新经典高等学校英语系列教程

丛书主编◎王立松　江滨　刘旸

U0829778

跨文化交际

主编◎周僡　耿艳梅　李秋然

Intercultural Communication

天津大学出版社
TIANJIN UNIVERSITY PRESS

图书在版编目（CIP）数据

跨文化交际 / 周僡，耿艳梅，李秋然主编. -- 天津 ：天津大学出版社，2025. 3. --（新经典高等学校英语系列教程 / 王立松，江滨，刘旸主编）. -- ISBN 978-7-5618-7892-7

Ⅰ. G115

中国国家版本馆CIP数据核字第20257JG683号

KUA WENHUA JIAOJI

本书为国家社会科学基金重大项目“区域国别学学科基础理论与方法研究”（项目编号：24&ZD316）阶段性成果

出版发行	天津大学出版社
地　　址	天津市卫津路92号天津大学内（邮编：300072）
电　　话	发行部：022-27403647
网　　址	www.tjupress.com.cn
印　　刷	廊坊市瑞德印刷有限公司
经　　销	全国各地新华书店
开　　本	787mm×1092mm　1/16
印　　张	9
字　　数	281千
版　　次	2025年3月第1版
印　　次	2025年3月第1次
定　　价	32.80元

前　言

随着构建人类命运共同体和共建“一带一路”等倡议的提出，中国与世界各国之间的经济文化交流更加密切。为促进中外文明融合发展，我国需要培养大量具有跨文化沟通和交际能力的国际化人才。跨文化人才需求对中国外语教学提出了新要求，对所有致力于为国育才的外语教师提出了新要求。天津大学作为中国近代第一所大学，承担着为国家培养具有家国情怀和全球视野的国际化人才的使命与责任。

为实现天津大学人才培养目标，外国语学院始终积极进行着外语教学改革。编者在教学改革中，分别给 2017、2019 和 2021 级的非英语专业本科生开设过“跨文化交际”课程。通过课程学习，学生对文化、跨文化交际等概念有了一定的了解，提高了跨文化交际意识，并对国内外文化有更加深刻的理解，对跨文化交际中存在的问题和障碍也有了一定的认识。部分选修此课程的同学，出国留学后适应目的国的文化相对顺利。

通过总结教学经验，编者以胡文仲的《跨文化交际学概论》和拉里 · 萨莫瓦尔等的《跨文化交际（影印改编版）》这两本经典教材为基础，并借鉴其他同类教材，结合出国研修经历，编写了此书。

本书注重理论与实践的结合，既涵盖了经典的如霍夫斯泰德的文化维度理论，又融入了对外汉语教师在诸多共建“一带一路”国家亲身经历的跨文化交际案例。学生在课堂上使用本书时，可以通过听讲、回答问题，与教师形成良好的互动，并通过小组活动参与案例情景下的角色扮演，获得接近实际的真实体验，加强对英语语言文化的认知与应用，并进行相应的思考与讨论。

本书共十个单元。第一单元介绍共建“一带一路”的发展和跨文化交际的意义。第二单元讲述语言和文化的影响力。第三单元和第四单元分别从言语交际和非言语交际两个方面讲述面对面跨文化交际中遇到的实际问题。第五单元和第六单元分别从跨性别文化交际和文化多样性方面介绍了多姿多彩的文化，以及文化多样性带来的负面影响，如文化休克。第七单元和第八单元分别讲述教育和商务中的文化差异。根据不同领域沟通中存在的障碍，第九章总结出跨文化交际中的一些共性问题，并在第十章给出克服沟通障碍、培养跨文化交际胜任力的方法和建议。

本书适合大学本科学生及对跨文化交际和对外汉语教学感兴趣的人员学习使用，可为读者培养自己的跨文化交际能力、参与国际交流活动提供帮助。

本书由周傈编写第一、七、八、九、十单元，耿艳梅编写第二、三、四单元，李秋然编写第五、六单元。本书从构思准备、组织编写到最后成书，得到天津大学外国语学院的全方位支持。在编写过程中，本书参考和引用了若干前人的研究成果，除直接引用者已在书中注明外，未能一一注明出处，在此一并向相关前辈学者、同行深表感谢！本书得以出版，要特别感谢天津大学出版社的大力支持，尤其衷心感谢各位编辑对本书提出的建设性意见以及为本书的出版付出的辛劳与努力！

由于编者水平有限，疏漏在所难免，真诚欢迎所有读者批评指正。

编者

2024 年 12 月于天津大学

Table of Contents

Unit 1

One World One Dream

Our most basic common link is that we all inhabit this planet.

— John F. Kennedy

Learning Objectives

At the end of this unit, you should be able to:

- understand the importance of intercultural communication;
- learn useful words and expressions related to globalization and intercultural communication;
- understand the features of communication.

Warm-up Activities

1 Case Study

Mr. Li, a Chinese teacher, was invited to attend an American friend's party when he was in the United States as a visiting scholar. At the party he ran into another American friend, Laura, who had once taught English in Tianjin for two years. They became so absorbed in recalling their respective teaching experiences in Tianjin that they did not notice how time had flown. Then, Laura said, "I am very interested in talking with you as we share much with each other, and I would like to invite you over for a talk at home in the near future." Mr. Li was pleased to accept the invitation. Soon Laura said, "I am leaving now and will contact you later." They said goodbye to each other. Mr. Li took what Laura said seriously and expected to see her again. He waited for several months, but never heard from Laura again, which prompted him to wonder why she did not keep her word or if he had misunderstood her.

1. ***What do you think of Laura's invitation? Is it a real invitation or a conversation closer?***
2. ***Identify a real invitation or not and tell your reasons for such choices. Tick the real ones.***

- ☐ Are you doing anything on weekend? Maybe we could hang out together?
- ☐ Would you like to have a talk on Friday night?
- ☐ I'm hosting a barbecue on Sunday. And I was wondering if you would like to join me.
- ☐ Do you wanna grab a bite after your work?
- ☐ Do you feel like coming to my home some day?
- ☐ How about grabbing coffee later?

2 Listen and Discuss

SCAN ME!

Good morning, ladies and gentlemen! And welcome to the third in our series of business seminars in the program — *Doing Business Abroad.* Today we are going to look for different culture awareness, that is, the fact that not everyone is British, not everyone speaks English, and not everyone does business in the British way. And why should they? If overseas business people are selling to us, then they will make every effort to speak English and to expect our traditions and methods. It is only polite for us to do the same when we visit them. It is not only polite. It is central if we want to sell British projects overseas.

First, a short quiz. Let's see how to cultivate where you are. Question 1: Where must you not drink alcohol on the first and seventh of every month? Question 2: Where should you never admire your host's positions? Question 3: How should you attract the waiter during a business lunch in banquet? And Question 4: Where should you try to make all your appointments either before 2:00 or after 5:30 p.m.?

(选自 2018 年 6 月大学英语六级考试听力)

1. *There are several errors in the above printed script. Listen carefully and find them.*

Para. 1

Error 1 ________________ Error 2 ________________ Error 3________________

Para. 2

Error 1 ________________ Error 2 ________________ Error 3________________

2. *What is the main theme of this third seminar?*

Text A

Does Intercultural Communication Matter?

1 In 2008 the Olympic Games were held in China for the first time. "One World One Dream" was the slogan for the Beijing 2008 Summer Olympic Games. It was announced as our beautiful wish that the world would be a harmonious family for people from different cultures.

2 In 2022, the Winter Olympic Games were held in China, which made Beijing the only city hold both the summer and winter Olympic Games. Building a community with a shared future is the dream all Chinese have for the future. Since the reform and opening-up in 1978, Chinese people have been working diligently to play an active part in the global village. With the economic and technological development in the past more than 4 decades, China has the confidence to forge ahead into a bright future where people from different continents work together for global peace and progress. Chinese people hold a strong belief for a harmonious world community in the ongoing trend of globalization.

3 **Globalization**

4 Globalization is the process of interaction and integration among people, companies, and governments worldwide. Its origins can be traced back to the 18th and 19th centuries due to advances in transportation and communication technology. Globalization is primarily an economic process of interaction and integration that is associated with social and cultural aspects.

5 Many historians agree that despite the fact that the large-scale globalization began in the 18th and 19th centuries, a form of globalization emerged with the rise of trade among neighboring countries, which could be dated far back to ancient times. In this sense, China was a major contributor to early globalization for its promoting the Silk Road.

6 The Silk Road

7 The Silk Road is named after the **lucrative** international trade in Chinese silk textiles that started during the Han Dynasty (206 BCE-220 CE). Using one single name for this intricate web of trade routes is a modern invention; the name Silk Road was coined by a German geographer **Ferdinand von Richthofen** in the late 19th century.

8 As an ancient trade route, the Silk Road linked the Western world with the Middle East and Asia. It was a major conduit for trade between the Roman Empire and China, later between medieval European kingdoms and China. Chinese merchants exported silk to Western buyers. From Rome and later from Christian kingdoms, wools, gold, and silver traveled eastward. Common goods such as salt and sugar were traded as well. In addition to economic trade, the Silk Road served as a means of carrying out cultural trade among the civilizations along its network. The movement of people, such as refugees, artists, craftsmen, missionaries, robbers, and **envoys**, resulted in the exchange of religions, art, languages, and new technologies.

9 Parts of the Silk Road survive in the form of a paved highway connecting **Pakistan** and China. The Silk Road also inspired China's Belt and Road Initiative(BRI), a global **infrastructure** development plan authored by Chinese government.

10 The Belt and Road Initiative (BRI)

11 In 2013, Chinese government proposed the Silk Road Economic Belt and the 21st-Century Maritime Silk Road successively in **Kazakhstan** and **Indonesia**. This is how the BRI, aimed at building a trade, investment, and infrastructure network that connects different regions along the ancient trade routes, took shape.

12 The term "belt" refers to overland infrastructure corridors linked to each other, which constitute the Silk Road Economic Belt component of BRI.

13 The term "road" refers to the sea route corridors, which constitute the 21st-Century Maritime Silk Road component of BRI.

14 Ten years on, the BRI has achieved more than connectivity. The Belt and Road cooperation, following the guiding principle of achieving shared growth through consulation and collaboration has grown into a global platform where countries along the routes work together to promote people's wellbeing and give a further boost to global development amid **daunting** challenges. The third Belt and Road Forum for International Cooperation was held in Beijing on 17-18 October, 2023. This event marks the 10th anniversary of the Belt and Road Initiative. Chinese President Xi Jinping attended the opening ceremony of the forum and delivered a keynote speech. He stressed again that we should advance modernization

of all countries, build an open, inclusive and interconnected world for common development, and jointly build a community with a shared future for mankind.

15 **Significance of Intercultural Awareness**

16 In the globalization era, with the promotion of BRI, Chinese people have more and more interactions with foreigners both at home and abroad. There are a large number of overseas students studying in Chinese universities, especially from the BRI participant countries. More and more Chinese people can afford to travel to foreign countries. Chinese college graduates, the future backbone of China's development, have greater possibility to participate in international business and engineering after graduation. Intercultural communicative activities therefore will be unavoidable for the young generations. However, even though the spatial distance between people can be easily shortened by modern transportation and communication technology, the psychological distance between people from different cultures can hardly be narrowed in a short period. Because the historical origins, social customs, value orientations, ways of thinking, social norms, etc. are deeply rooted in various cultures of different nations, which are potential obstacles to **preclude** people from efficient communication and mutual understanding. What's worse, possible cultural conflicts may bring unnecessary disasters to people with good intentions. It is hence necessary to cultivate the intercultural awareness among young generations in Chinese colleges and universities.

17 Courses related to intercultural communication have been available to most students majoring in international business, tourism, and foreign language study in recent years. To better represent China and tell Chinese stories, college students of all majors are encouraged to foster intercultural awareness and accumulate knowledge about various cultures in our shared community. Only by understanding and respecting the diversity of human civilizations, can we reach the goal of "One World One Dream".

lucrative 获利丰厚的	Kazakhstan 哈萨克斯坦
Ferdinand von Richthofen 费迪南·冯·李希霍芬（1833—1905，德国著名地理学家、地质学家）	Indonesia 印度尼西亚
envoy 特使，使者	daunting 使人畏惧的，使人气馁的
Pakistan 巴基斯坦	preclude 阻止，妨碍（preclude sb. from）
infrastructure 基础设施	

Reading Comprehension

Each of the following statements contains information in Text A. Decide whether the statement is true (T) or false (F) based on the text.

1. The large-scale globalization began in the 18th and 19th centuries.
2. There is the example of the famous "Silk Road" in which people of Asia, Africa and America interacted and communicated with each other for trade.
3. The term "road" refers to the sea route corridors, which constitute the 21st-Century Maritime Silk Road component of BRI.
4. The name Silk Road was coined by a Greek geographer Ferdinand von Richthofen.

Text B

What Is Intercultural Communication?

1 Intercultural communication is a discipline that studies communication across different cultures and social groups, or how culture affects communication. It describes the wide range of communication processes and problems that naturally appear within an organization or social context made up of individuals from different religious, social, ethnic, and educational backgrounds. In this sense, it seeks to understand how people from different countries and cultures act, communicate, and perceive the world around them. Intercultural communication focuses on the recognition and respect of those with cultural differences. The goal is mutual adaptation between two or more distinct cultures which leads to **biculturalism/multiculturalism** rather than complete **assimilation**. It promotes the development of cultural sensitivity and allows for empathic understanding across different cultures.

2 As a discipline, intercultural communication originally prospered in the United States. Many scholars agree that **Edward T. Hall** ignited the interest in the study on intercultural communication by his book *The Silent Language* published first in 1959. In 1980s, Chinese scholars began to have relevant studies and books on intercultural communication. Nowadays, many universities have courses on intercultural communication to promote the intercultural sensitivity of college students. Intercultural communication plays a role in social sciences such as anthropology, cultural studies, linguistics, psychology, and communication studies. Intercultural

communication is also referred to as the base for international businesses.

3 Intercultural communication is the idea of knowing how to communicate within different parts of the world to avoid cultural misunderstandings. Many cultures — such as Japanese, go to great lengths not to be direct. The risk of disharmony with other group members is too great to be outspoken. It's better to agree to somebody in face and negotiate with them afterwards than to blatantly disagree. Direct communicators like Americans in general, consider this indirectness deceptive, two-faced and lacking in integrity.

4 There are many obstacles to effective intercultural communication. Many people naively assume there are sufficient similarities among peoples of the world to make communication easy. They expect that simply being human and having common requirements of food, shelter, security, and so on makes everyone alike. Unfortunately, they overlook the fact that the forms of adaptation to these common biological and social needs and the values, beliefs, and attitudes surrounding them are vastly different from culture to culture. The biological commonalties are not much help when it comes to communication, where we need to exchange ideas and information, find ways to live and work together, or just make the kind of impression we want to make.

5 Some people will cling to just one meaning of a word or phrase in the new language, regardless of connotation or context. The variations in possible meaning, especially when inflection and tone are varied, are so difficult to cope with that they are often waved aside. This complacency will stop a search for understanding.

6 The misinterpretation of observable nonverbal signs and symbols — such as gestures, postures, and other body movements — is a definite communication barrier. But it is possible to learn the meanings of these observable messages, usually in informal rather than formal ways. It is more difficult to understand the less obvious unspoken codes of the other cultures, such as the handling of time and spatial relationships and the subtle signs of respect of formality.

7 Some major obstacles will be further discussed later in Unit 9.

8 There is no easy solution and there is not only one way to realize effective intercultural communication. However, when involved in an intercultural communicative situation, some basic principles are always helpful:

9 Show respect and positive regard for the other person.

10 Behave in ways that show one understands the point of view of others.

11 Initiate ideas that encourage problem solving activities.

12 React to new situations with little discomfort.

13 Respond to others in descriptive, non-judgmental ways.

biculturalism/multiculturalism 二元文化 / 多元文化	blatantly 公然地，公开地
assimilation 同化	wave aside 拒绝考虑或回应，置之不理
Edward T. Hall 爱德华·霍尔（1914 — 2009，美国人类学家，被称为“系统地研究跨文化传播活动的第一人”）	complacency 自满，自鸣得意
go to great lengths 竭尽全力（做某事）	

Reading Comprehension

Which of the following barriers to intercultural communication has been mentioned in Text B? Tick all you can find.

- ☐ Tendency to evaluate.
- ☐ Open-mindedness.
- ☐ Stereotypes.
- ☐ Nonverbal misinterpretations.
- ☐ High anxiety.
- ☐ Language differences.
- ☐ Assumption of similarities.
- ☐ Racism.
- ☐ Problem-solving.
- ☐ Generalizing.

Banked Cloze

Fill in the blanks by selecting suitable words from the word bank. You may not use any of the words more than once.

A. conflicts	B. concerted	C. coexist	D. decisive	E. inability
F. intriguing	G. name-calling	H. societies	I. subcultures	J. values

The growth of intercultural communication as a field of study is based on a view of history that clearly demonstrates people and cultures have been troubled by a persistent 1 ____________ to understand and get along with groups and 2 ____________ removed by space, ideology, appearance, and behavior from their own.

What is [3] ____________ about many of human civilization's failures is that they appear to be personal as well as global. The story of humankind is punctuated with instances of face-to-face [4] ____________ as well as international misunderstanding — major and minor quarrels that range from simple [5] ____________ to isolationism or even armed conflict.

It is obvious that increased contact with other cultures and [6] ____________ makes it imperative for us to make a [7] ____________ effort to understand and get along with people whose beliefs and backgrounds may be vastly different from our own. The ability, through increased awareness and understanding, to peacefully [8] ____________ with people who do not necessarily share our lifestyles or [9] ____________ could benefit us not only in our own neighborhoods but could be the [10] ____________ factor in maintaining world peace.

Text C

Understanding Communication

1 To reach the goal of "One World One Dream", we need to have effective intercultural communication. The key elements involved are "culture" and "communication". We begin by introducing communication and move to culture in Unit 2.

2 Communication is the basis of all human contact. Today contact may take a variety of forms, such as meeting people face-to-face, exchanging ideas via social networks and other media methods. What matters is not the tool but rather the idea that you are sharing part of yourself with another human being. Communication is one of the most rewarding experiences people can have. It is one of the major ways you fulfill a social component within yourself. Linking with others allows you to experience a sense of inclusion and affection.

3 Not only does communication allow you to make human connections, but it also assists in collecting data about other people. Personal experience reveals that when you meet someone for the first time, gathering information about that individual is necessary and begins immediately. That information serves two purposes. First, it enables you to learn about the other person so that you may better understand the messages they are producing. Second, it assists in deciding how to present yourself to that person. These judgments affect everything from the topics selected to talk about to whether you decide to continue the conversation or terminate it. This information is essential in intercultural communication because in many instances you

are dealing with "strangers".

4 It is difficult to define the term "communication" because it has been used in a variety of ways for varied and sometimes inconsistent purposes. Generally speaking, communication can refer to a dynamic, symbolic, **transactional** and contextual process in which people create shared meanings or messages.

5 Communication can be classified based on whether information is exchanged between humans, members of other species, or non-living entities such as computers. For human communication, a central contrast is between verbal and nonverbal communication. Verbal communication involves the exchange of messages in linguistic forms. This can happen through natural languages, like English or Chinese, or through artificial languages, like **Esperanto**. Verbal communication includes spoken and written messages as well as the use of sign language. Nonverbal communication happens without the use of a linguistic system. There are many forms of nonverbal communication, for example, using body language, body position, touch, and intonation. Both verbal communication and nonverbal communication will be illustrated in detail in the following units (Unit 3 and Unit 4).

6 From Aristotle through to modern semiotics, all theories of communication were based on a single model called the "code model". According to the code model, communication is achieved by encoding and decoding messages. A widely quoted diagram of Shannon and Weaver shows how communication can be achieved by use of a code:

7 The Shannon-Weaver Model (Fig 1.1) focuses on how a message is first translated into a signal and then back into a message. Communication is achieved by encoding a message, which cannot travel, into a signal, which can, and by decoding this signal at the receiving end. Noise along the channel can destroy or distort the signal. Otherwise, as long as the devices are in order and the codes are identical at both ends, successful communication is guaranteed.

8 As Shannon was an engineer, this model was first made to improve technical communication, mainly for telephonic communication. It was made to maximize telephone capacity with minimum noise. Later, Weaver applied it for all kind of communications to develop effective communication and the model became famous as Shannon-Weaver Model.

9 Another early model, developed in the

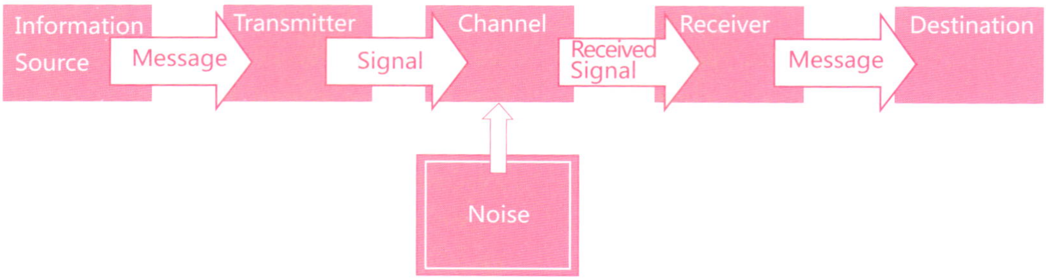

Fig 1.1　Shannon-Weaver Model

middle of the 20th century is Lasswell's model (Fig 1.2), which is a linear transmission model as well. Lasswell's Model is based on five fundamental questions: "Who?", "Says What?", "In Which Channel?", "To Whom?", and "With What Effect?". The goal of these questions is to identify the basic components involved in the communicative process: the communicator, the message, the medium, the receiver, and the effect. Lasswell's Model was initially only conceived as a model of mass communication, but it has been applied to other fields as well. Some theorists, like Richard Braddock, have expanded it by including additional questions, like "Under What Circumstances?" and "For What Purpose?".

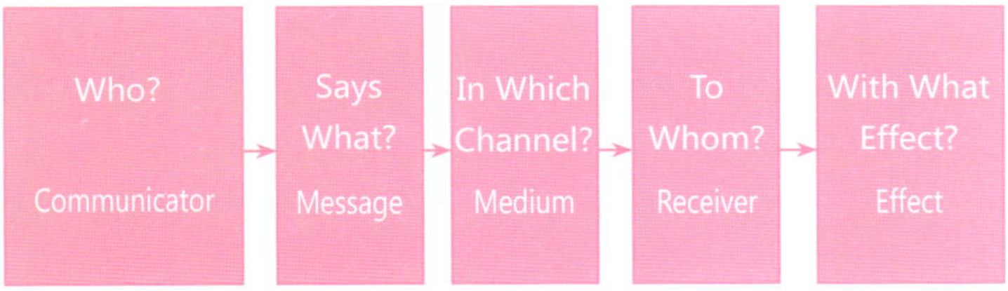

Fig 1.2 Lasswell's Model

10 The models of communication are usually presented visually in the form of diagrams showing the basic components and their interaction. Their goal is to provide a simplified overview of its main components. This makes it easier for researchers to formulate hypotheses, apply communication-related concepts to real-world cases, and test predictions. However, it is often argued that many models lack the conceptual complexity needed for a comprehensive understanding of all the essential aspects of communication. Especially when two parities in a communication are from distinct cultures, effective communication is about more than just exchanging information. It's about understanding the emotion and intention behind the information.

11 To better understand communication hence to improve its effectiveness, the characteristics and some misconceptions will be discussed in the following part (Fig 1.3).

12 **Communication is a dynamic process.**

13 Communication is like a motion picture, not a single snapshot. A word or action does

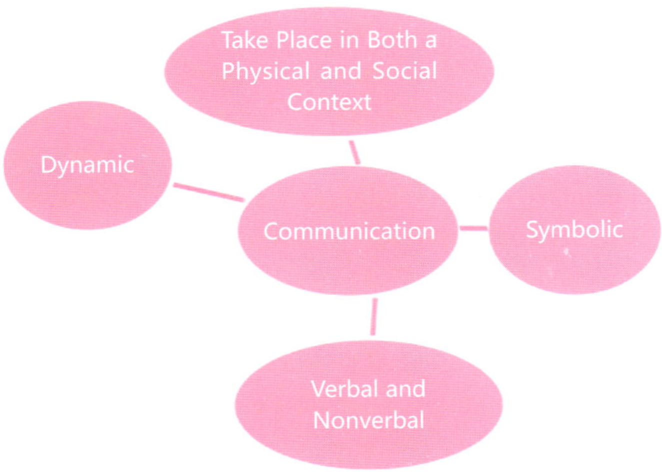

Fig 1.3 Features of Communication

not stay frozen when you communicate. It is immediately replaced with yet another word or action. Once a word or action is produced, it cannot be **retracted**. Sending and receiving messages involves a host of variables, all in operation at the same time. Each of the parties of the transaction is reacting to the others by seeing, listening, talking, thinking, and perhaps smiling and touching the other, all at once.

14 **Communication is symbolic.**

15 You cannot access the internal thoughts and feelings of other human beings, you can only infer what they are experiencing by what you see and hear. Those inferences are drawn from the symbols people produce. In human communication, a symbol is an expression that stands for or represents something else. Although those symbols may be **spontaneous** and nonintentional (someone sneezes, and you infer they have a cold) or intentional (someone tells you they have a cold), both involve your attaching meaning to a symbolic event generated by another person. In many ways, this act of attaching meaning to symbols is at the core of human communication. Other animals may engage in some forms of communication and even make use of some symbols, but none has the unique communicative capabilities found among humans. Through millions of years of physical evolution and thousands of years of cultural development, humans are able to generate, receive, store, and **manipulate** symbols. This sophisticated system allows people to use symbols — sounds, marks on paper, letters on the screen of a cell phone, sculptures, **Braille**, gestures, or paintings — to represent something else. Reflect for a moment on the wonderful gift you have allows you to hear the words "The kittens look like cotton balls", and, like magic, you have an image in your head. Because the image you **conjure up** for "kittens" and "cotton balls" is inside of you, it is essential to remember that each person "defines" those words and phrases from his or her own cultural perspective. Therefore, it is always important to keep in mind that language symbols are no more consistent or precise than the experience, values, and belief systems of the people using them.

16 In terms of intercultural communication, it is important to keep in mind the fact that the symbols you use are **discretionary** and subjective. There is no innate connection between the symbols and their **referents**. The relationships are **arbitrary** and usually shift from culture to culture. In short, although all cultures use symbols, they usually assign their own meanings to them. Not only do Spanish speakers say "perro" for "dog", but the mental image they form when they hear the sound is probably quite different from the one Mandarin Chinese speakers form when they hear "gou", their word for "dog". In addition to having different meanings for symbols, cultures also use these symbols for different purposes.

17 **Communication is contextual.**

18 Communication does not occur in a vacuum. As previously noted, communication is a dynamic process and composed of many ingredients. One of those ingredients is context. This implies that setting and environment

help determine the words and actions you generate and the meanings you give to the symbols you receive. In addition, whether consciously or subconsciously, context plays a role in establishing which behavior is favored and which is deemed inappropriate. Attire, language, nonverbal behavior, topic selection, and vocabulary are all adapted to the context. Reflect for a moment on how differently you would behave in each of the following settings: a classroom, a church, a courtroom, a funeral, a wedding, a sporting event, a hospital, or a nightclub. For example, a male would not attend a university lecture, even in hot weather, without wearing a shirt. However, at a football stadium, you might find a whole row of males without shirts on (possibly with letters painted on their chests), and this would be socially acceptable.

19 Even the words we exchange are contextual. The simple phrase "How are you?" shifts meaning as you move from place to place and person to person. To a friend, it can be a straightforward expression used as a greeting. Yet during a doctor's appointment, the same three words ("How are you?") uttered by the **physician** call for a detailed response regarding your physical condition.

20 In most instances, the context involves four aspects: the number of people who are interacting, the environmental context, the occasion, and the time.

21 **Communication is complex.**

22 Communication is complex in that it can involve controlling, informing, persuading, and relating to others. Reflect for a moment on all the bodily and mental activity that accompanies even the simple act of saying hello to a friend. From the stimulation of your nerve endings to the secretion of chemicals in your brain to the moving of your lips to produce sound, thousands of components are in operation (most of them at the same time). Not only are there countless biological and physical factors coming into play all at once, but there are also many elements to each person's personality.

23 For example, during a single interaction there are six "people" involved: (1) the person that you imagine yourself to be, (2) the other person as you perceive him or her, (3)your notion of what you believe the other person thinks of you, (4) the other person as he or she supposes he or she is, (5) how the other person perceives you, and (6) the other person's notion of how he or she believes you perceive him or her.

24 Communication becomes even more complex when cultural dimensions are added. Although all cultures use symbols to share their realities, the specific realities and the symbols employed are often quite different. In one culture, you smile in a casual manner as a form of greeting; in another, you bow formally in silence; and in yet another, you acknowledge your friend with a full embrace.

transactional	事务性的，业务处理的	conjure up	使浮现于脑海，使想起
Esperanto	世界语（一种逻辑化、包含着多种主体语言所公认的词根、相对容易学习的语言。支持者设想其是在一个统一的世界中使用的语言）	discretionary	便宜行事的，酌情行事的
retract	撤回，收回	referent	所指对象，指示物
spontaneous	自发的，非筹划安排的	arbitrary	任意的，随意的
manipulate	使用，操纵	physician	医师，内科医生
Braille	布莱叶盲文		

Reading Comprehension

Each of the following statements summarizes information in Text C. Decide whether the statement is true (T) or false (F) based on the text.

1. The Lasswell's Model focuses on how a message is first translated into a signal and then back into a message.
2. Communication is a dynamic process in which people attempt to share their internal states with other people through the use of symbols.
3. The components of communication include source, encoding, message, channel, receiver, decoding, feedback and noise.

Suggestions for Further Reading

Unit 2

Language and Culture

The sum of human wisdom is not contained in any one single language, and no single language is capable of expressing all forms and degrees of human comprehension.

— Ezra Pound

Learning Objectives

At the end of this unit, you should be able to:

- know the importance of language;
- better understand the relationship between language and culture;
- learn something about Sapir-Whorf Hypothesis;
- know the definitions, functions and characteristics of culture;
- learn about Hofstede's dimensions of culture and high- and low-context cultures.

Warm-up Activities

1 Case Study

An American businessman is reviewing an important contract with his Japanese counterpart.

"We've got to work together," the American says.

"Hai (はい, "yes" in Japanese)," the Japanese smiles.

"We're going to try for a 50-50 partnership," the American says.

"Hai."

"We will use American know-how and Japanese work force."

"Hai."

After this exchange, the American executive might very well assume he has a hard and fast agreement.

Question:

Do you agree that the agreement is a hard and fast one? Why?

2 Proverbs and Idioms

Match the Chinese proverbs or idioms in Column A with its equivalent English version in Column B.

Column A

(1) 不入虎穴，焉得虎子。

(2) 掌握另一门语言，拥有第二个灵魂。

(3) 谋事在人，成事在天。

(4) 智者千虑，必有一失。

(5) 凡人皆有得意之日。

(6) 不了解外语的人也无法真正了解自己的语言。

Column B

a. Every dog has its day.
b. Even Homer sometimes nods.
c. Man proposes, God disposes.
d. Go to the sea, if you would fish well.
e. To have another language is to possess a second soul.
f. Those who know nothing of foreign languages know nothing of their own.

Text A

The Importance of Language

1 The term language is far more complex than we imagine. Language is a symbolic system, and when put together according to a certain set of rules, it conveys meanings to its speakers. Being an extremely important way for human interaction, language expresses and **embodies** cultural reality and is **inextricably entwined** with culture; language is an important way to transmit culture, and is the carrier of culture which in turn is the content of language.

2 The importance of language to the study of intercultural communication is clearly captured in the American poet **Ralph Waldo Emerson**'s "Language is the **archives** of history." It is generally held that language is the major vehicle for human thought, and it is largely through language that we pass on our cultural heritage from one generation to the next.

3 The richness and expressive **versatility** of language was recognized by **Paul Tillich** when he observed that "language has created the word 'loneliness' to express the pain of being alone and the word 'solitude' to express the joy of being alone". The meanings attached to any given word in all languages are, however, totally **arbitrary**.

4 For example, the word cow has no particular connection to that large animal that the English refer to as a cow. The word cow does not look like, sound like, or have any particular physical connection to a cow. The only explanation for the use of the word is that somewhere during the evolution of the English language someone decided that the word cow would be used to refer to a large **domesticated** animal that gives an abundant quantity of milk. Other languages use totally different, and equally arbitrary words to describe this same animal. Take a Chinese character "牛"(niú) for example (Fig 2.1). "牛", a pictograph (Xiang Xing Zi, 象形字), only represents part of the animal — the head, as illustrated in Fig 2.1. With its evolution from  in the Oracle Bone Inscription (Jia Gu Wen, 甲骨文) to  in the Bronze Inscription (Jin Wen, 金文) to  in the Small Seal Script (Xiao Zhuan, 小篆) to **牛** in

Fig 2.1 Forms of the Chinese Character "牛" in Different Scripts

the Clerical Script (Li Shu, 隶书) and 牛 in the Regular Script (Kai Shu, 楷书), the character resembles the shape of the head increasingly less. So the Chinese characters are also arbitrary.

5 All people, drawing on their backgrounds, decide what a word means. People have similar meanings only to the extent that they have had or can anticipate similar experiences. The word grass, to one person, might mean something in front of the house that is green, has to be watered, and must be mowed once a week; to another person, it may mean something that is rolled in paper and smoked.

6 Language is extremely important to human interaction because it is how we reach out to make contact with our surroundings. If we were to survey a normal day, we would soon see that we use words for a wide variety of purposes. We may use language when we first awake, "Good morning!", face to face or via WeChat. We use words to persuade, to exchange ideas, to express views, to seek information, and to express feelings.

7 We employ words to relate to the past, that is, to talk about something that has already happened, "Let me tell you about the horrible dream I had last night."

8 We use words so that we can exert some control over the present, "Please pass the salt and pepper." We each seek to affect our environment, to influence many of the daily situations in which we find ourselves.

9 We also use words to form images of the future, "I have to meet with Susie at work today, but I dread seeing her, because I know she's going to be upset about the changes I'm making in our work schedule."

10 Language enables humans to send literally an **infinite** array of messages, including abstract ideas, highly technical information, and subtle shades of meaning. Starting with a limited number of sounds, human languages are capable of producing an infinite number of meanings by combining sounds and words into meanings that may have never been sent before.

11 To illustrate, by combining a series of words in a certain order, we can convey a unique message that has never been previously uttered, "I think that the woman named Clela with the bright orange hair left her leather handbag in the 1951 Studebaker that was involved in a hit-and-run accident later in the day." This productive capacity of human language illustrates how efficient and flexible human communication can be.

12 Our ability to use words is indeed a remarkable gift. Over two thousand years ago, the Athenian poet **Aristophanes** glorified

the beauty of words, "By words the mind is winged." Everything that we are is inside our body. Most of this internal state is residing in our brain. Our beliefs, values, attitudes, world views, emotions, and myriad other aspects of ourselves and personalities are locked up inside of us.

embody	体现，包含，代表（思想或品质），具体表现	Paul Tillich	保罗·田立克（1886—1965，德裔美籍基督教存在主义哲学家、神学家）
inextricably	密不可分地，不可分开地	arbitrary	任意的，武断的，专横的，随心所欲的
entwine	缠绕，纠缠，与……密切相关（或紧密相连）	domesticated	驯养的，家养的，驯化的
Ralph Waldo Emerson	拉尔夫·华尔多·爱默生（1803—1882，美国超验主义运动领袖）	infinite	无限的，极大的，无穷尽的
archive	档案	Aristophanes	阿里斯托芬（约公元前446年—前385年，古希腊喜剧作家、诗人）
versatility	多才多艺，技术全面，用途广泛		

Short-answer Questions

Please answer the following questions according to what you've learned from the textbook.

1. Why is language so important to human beings?
2. Try to find out the functions of language as many as possible and provide examples to illustrate these functions.

Reading Comprehension

Each of the following statements contains information in Text A. Decide whether the statement is true (T) or false (F) based on the text.

1. The most distinctive feature of being human is the capacity to create and use language and other symbolic forms.
2. Language is the carrier for human thought, and it is largely through language that cultural heritage is transmitted from generation to generation.
3. Language serves the social function of communication, but it has difficulty identifying social groups.
4. Language enables humans to send literally an infinite array of messages, not including abstract ideas though.
5. The meanings attached to any given word in all languages are arbitrary.

Text B

Language and Its Cultural Influence

1 It is impossible to separate our use of language from our culture. Language is a set of symbols and the rules for combining those symbols that are used and understood by a large community of people. When we study another language, we soon discover that not only are the symbols (words) and sounds for those symbols different, but also are the rules (**phonology**, grammar, **syntax**, and intonation) for using those symbols and sounds.

2 Word differences are obvious in various languages. In English, people live in a house; in Spanish, people live in a casa; in Thai, people live in a baan; and in Chinese, people live in "房子" (fáng zi). In English, people drink coffee, while in Chinese, people drink "咖啡"(kā fēi).

3 Phonology also varies culturally. In English, there are 21 consonant sounds and 5 vowels that combine to form 38 various sounds. The Filipino language has 16 consonants and 10 vowels forming 26 phonemes. Portuguese has 21 consonants and 13 vowels that form 34 basic phonemes.

4 Grammatical structures are unique to each language as well. In English, there are singular and plural nouns and pronouns, but in Korean, the distinction between singular and plural is made by the context of the sentence. In English, verb tenses express contrast between past, present, and future acts, but in Vietnamese, the same verb reflects all three and the time of the action is inferred from the context.

5 Syntax, or the word order and structure of sentences, also varies depending on the language. The normal word order for simple sentences in Filipino is the reverse of that in English. For example, the English sentence "The teacher died." would be "Died the teacher." or "Namatay ang guro." in Filipino. In English, the subject is followed by a verb and then an object, but in Korean, the subject is followed by the object and then the verb. So in English we might say, "The dog bites the bone." but in Korean, "Dog bone bites." would be correct.

6 To understand the effects of language on intercultural communication, questions such as the following must be explored.

7 ★ How do initial experiences with language shape or influence the way a person thinks?

8 ★ Do the categories of a language — its words, grammar, and usage — influence how people think and behave? More specifically, consider the following question: Does a person growing up in Saudi Arabia, who learns to speak and write Arabic, "see" and "experience" the world differently than a person who grows up speaking and writing Tagalog in the Philippines?

9 **The Sapir-Whorf Hypothesis**

10 Language and its cultural influence are exemplified in the Sapir-Whorf Hypothesis, which in essence states that language is a guide to "social reality". This hypothesis implies that language is not simply a means of reporting

experience but, more importantly, it is a way of defining experience.

11 The best-known example of vocabulary differences associated with the Sapir-Whorf Hypothesis is the large number of words for snow in the Eskimo language. Depending on whom you ask, there are from seven to fifty different words for snow in the Inuktitut language. For example, there are words that **differentiate** falling snow (gana) and fully fallen snow (akilukak). The English language has fewer words for snow and no terms for many of the distinctions made by Eskimos.

12 The issue raised by the Sapir-Whorf Hypothesis is whether the person who grows up speaking Inuktitut actually **perceives** snow differently than one who grows up in southern California and may only know snow by secondhand descriptions. More importantly, could the southern Californian who lives with the Inuit in Alaska learn to differentiate all of the variations of snow and to use the specific Eskimo words appropriately?

13 The firm version of the Sapir-Whorf Hypothesis suggests that linguistic differences are accompanied by **perceptual** differences so that the English speaker looks at snow differently than the Eskimo speaker.

14 Although complete acceptance of the Sapir-Whorf Hypothesis may be **controversial**, its application to culture and language is clear: language is a reflection of culture, and culture is a reflection of language.

15 Later on, the Sapir-Whorf Hypothesis (Table 2.1) was modified and came in two versions, namely the firm version and the weak version. The firm version holds that the language patterns determine people's thinking and behavior, therefore it is also known as linguistic determinism. The weak version proclaims that the structure of the language people habitually use influences the ways they think and behave, i.e. different languages offer people different ways of expressing the world around, they think and speak differently, which is also known as linguistic relativity.

Table 2.1 Sapir-Whorf Hypothesis

Firm Version (Linguistic Determinism)	Weak Version (Linguistic Relativity)
Language determines thought and behavior.	Language influences thought and behavior.

phonology 音系，音系学	differentiate 区分，区别，辨别，（尤指不公正地）区别对待
syntax 句法，句法规则	perceive 感知，认为，察觉到，意识到
Sapir-Whorf Hypothesis 萨丕尔-沃尔夫假说	perceptual 感知的，知觉的
hypothesis 假设，（有少量事实依据但未被证实的）假说，（凭空的）猜想	controversial 有争议的，引起争论的

Reading Comprehension

Which of the following statements can describe language and its cultural influence as mentioned in Text B? Tick all you can find.

- ☐ Vocabulary varies among different cultures.
- ☐ Phonology varies culturally.
- ☐ Grammatical structures are unique to each language.
- ☐ Syntax, or the word order and structure of sentences, also varies culturally.
- ☐ Language also has a major impact on the way an individual perceives and conceptualizes the world.
- ☐ There is a large number of words for snow in the Eskimo language.
- ☐ Navaho people say "One moves into clothing." to mean "to put on clothes".
- ☐ In the islands, there are numerous words for camel.
- ☐ The worlds in which different societies live are similar, merely with different labels attached.
- ☐ Language is a reflection of culture, and vice versa.

Banked Cloze

Fill in the blanks by selecting suitable words from the word bank. You may not use any of the words more than once.

A. reflect	B. conceptualize	C. linguistic	D. persuade	E. enriched
F. subtle	G. recognition	H. glorify	I. relative	J. presupposition

It is commonly observed that the manner in which an idea or "fact" is stated affects the way we 1 ____________ the idea. Words shape our lives. The advertising world is a prime example of the use of language to shape, 2 ____________, and dissuade. "Weasel words" (含糊的词语) tend to 3 ____________ very ordinary products into those that are "sparkling" or "refreshing". In the case of food that has been sapped of most of its nutrients by the manufacturing process, we are told that these products are now "4 ____________" and "fortified". A foreigner in the United States once remarked that in the United States there are no "small" eggs, only "medium", "large", "extra-large", and "jumbo" (特大的).

Words are not the only 5 ____________ category affecting thought. The way a sentence is structured will affect nuances of meaning. It has been discovered that 6 ____________ differences in the structure of questions can affect the answer a person gives. For example, upon viewing a film of an automobile accident, subjects were asked questions like "Did you see the broken headlight?" in some cases, and in other cases "Did you see a broken headlight?". Questions using tended to produce more false 7 ____________ of events. That is, the presence of the definite article led subjects to believe that there was a broken headlight, whether they saw it or not. Similar results were found for questions like "Did you see some people watching the accident?" vs. "Did you see any people watching the accident?" or even for questions containing a 8 ____________: "How fast was the car going when it hit the stop sign?" (presupposing both the existence of a stop sign and that the car hit a stop sign, whether the subject actually saw it or not).

A question emerges from such observations. Does language 9 ____________ a cultural world view or does language actually shape the world view? Today many scholars have little concern about a debate over whether a language shapes thought or thought shapes language. They are more concerned, and rightly so, with the fact that language and culture interact, that world views among cultures differ, and that the language used to express that world view may be 10 ____________ and specific to that view.

Discussion

1. What do you think of Sapir-Whorf Hypothesis? Please provide an example to support your idea.
2. When people from different cultures are using the same word or discussing the same thing, for example, a cow, a dragon or a phoenix, will there be no misunderstanding? Why or why not?

Text C

Unveiling the Enigma of Culture

1 **What is culture all about?**

2 Culture originated from the Latin word cultura, cultra or cultus, which is from the verb colere, denoting to till (as in to till the soil or land), so its root meaning is "the cultivation of the soil". People learn to think, feel, believe, and act as they do because of the messages that have been communicated to them, and those messages all bear the stamp of culture.

3 Edward T. Hall concluded that "there is not

one aspect of human life that is not touched and altered by culture". In many ways, Hall is correct: culture is everything and everywhere. And more importantly, culture governs and defines the conditions and circumstances under which various messages may or may not be sent, noticed, or interpreted. Remember, we are not born knowing how to dress, what toys to play with, what to eat, which gods to worship, or how to spend our money and our time. Culture is both teacher and textbook. From how much eye contact we employ in conversations to explanations of why we get sick, culture plays a dominant role in our lives. Many definitions have been suggested for culture, as the American anthropologists Alfred L. Kroeber and Clyde Kluckhohn (1952) reviewed 164 concepts and definitions of culture, ranging from all-encompassing ones ("it is everything") to narrower ones ("it is opera, art, and ballet"). Culture is often compared to an iceberg or an onion, manifesting culture's different layers in depth (Fig 2.2).

Fig 2.2 The Cultural Iceberg

4 Culture is, put simply, a learned set of shared interpretations about beliefs, values, norms and social practices, which affect the behaviors of a relatively large group of people. It can also be summarized that culture involves at least three components, namely, what people think, what they do, and the material products they produce (Fig 2.3).

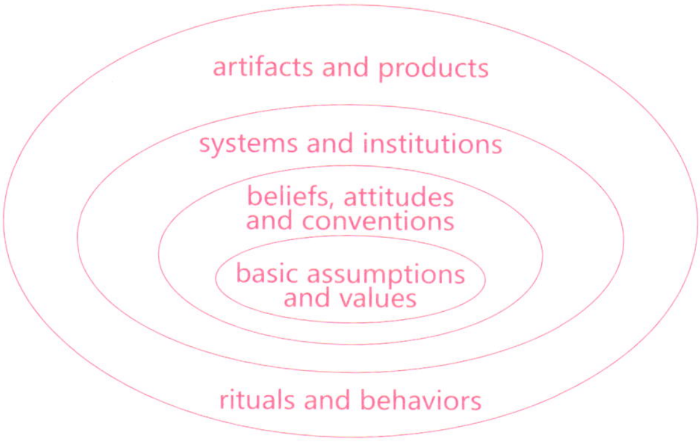

Fig 2.3 The Cultural Onion

5 **Characteristics of culture**

6 *Culture is learned behavior.*

7 Patterns of culture are not inherent with any individual. They are acquired through the process of learning or interacting with the individual's environment. The learning environment includes the family, neighborhood, schools, social groups, physical surroundings, etc. If the environment is different, the culture that each individual learns or acquires will be different too.

8 Think of some examples in your life or others' experience to illustrate this point.

9 *Culture is usually acquired unconsciously.*

10 The learning of culture is usually done unconsciously. Our relationship with culture is like that between birds and the sky, fish and water or people and air. Only when we are deprived of our own culture or put into a completely new culture can we realize the importance of culture to us. Without culture we cannot survive. Since culture is often learned unconsciously, we often fail to account for our behavior. In intercultural studies, we should make deliberate effort to understand how culture influences our own behavior as well as that of other people.

11 *Culture is shared among its members.*

12 The learned cultural patterns are shared by the members of the same group or society. When we say two individuals come from the same culture, we assume they share the same patterns of living: the same set of symbols for communication, the same rules of speaking, the same idea about what can be eaten as food, the same belief about nature and man, and so on. Within the same system, individuals can easily understand one another and adjust themselves to their surroundings.

13 *Culture is persistent and enduring.*

14 Culture is not created and developed overnight. It is the deposit of human knowledge and collection of both material and non-material wealth created by man over the long process of human civilization. This nature of culture gives continuity to the development of a culture and provides reinforcement to its members in their lifetime learning of the culture.

15 *Culture manifests itself both implicitly and explicitly.*

16 Some aspects of culture are easily

observable and some are not. The ways of dressing, talking, and working are readily noticeable, but the ideas and motivations underlying these superficial behaviors are generally unrecognized. The study of culture and its people should involve not only the learning of the explicit rules but also those implicit beliefs, values and attitudes that relate to them.

17 *Culture is adaptive and dynamic.*

18 Any great inventions and progress of mankind will bring about changes in people's ideas, way of life, mode of behavior, etc. These changes often take place on the superficial levels of a culture, while the deep structures i.e. ideological perceptions, values and value orientations, world views and beliefs, are likely to stay or change slowly. Therefore, the study of culture should take a dynamic perspective.

19 *Culture is relational.*

20 Any culture is an integrated entity. All the components of culture are interrelated. The change of one aspect of culture will definitely bring about changes in other aspects. Therefore, a relational approach should be adopted in the study of culture and people. Only in this way can we gain a true understanding of a culture and its people.

(Adapted from L. A. Samovar et al., *Communication between Cultures*, Chapter 2)

Short-answer Questions

Please answer the following questions according to what you've learned from the textbook.

1. What's your definition of culture? Provide one type of patterns, symbols, behaviors, beliefs, artifacts… that you believe is of Chinese culture and foreign culture.
2. What do you think are the characteristics of culture? Please use examples to illustrate "Culture is usually acquired unconsciously".

Translation

Translate the following definitions of culture into Chinese.

1. Culture consists of patterns, explicit and implicit, of and for behavior acquired and transmitted by symbols, constituting the distinctive achievement of human groups, including their embodiments in artifacts; the essential core of culture consists of traditional ideas and especially their attached values. (by Arthur Kroeber & Clyde Kluckhohn)

____

____

____

____

2. Culture is a system of shared beliefs, values, customs, behaviors and artifacts that the members of a society use to cope with their world and with one another, and that are transmitted from generation to generation through learning. (by Daniel Bates & Fred Plog)

Text D

Multi-facets of Culture

1 Regarding the hard-to-define term culture, many theories are proposed by different scholars. We choose two most influential ones by Edward T. Hall and Geert Hofstede respectively.

2 **High-context and Low-context Cultures**

3 Edward T. Hall remarks that meaning and context are **inextricably** bound up with each other; human communication is dependent on the context in which it occurs. Communicative context refers to the information that surrounds an event, which is composed of the physical, social, and interpersonal environments.

4 Hall then defines the two key terms in the following manner. A high-context (HC) communication or message is one in which most of the information is either in the physical context or internalized in the person, while very little is in the coded, explicit, transmitted part of the message. A low-context (LC) communication is just the opposite; i.e., the majority of the information is vested in the explicit code, in other words, the information is verbalized.

5 Hall categorizes cultures as being either high or low context, maintaining that although no culture exists exclusively at one end of the scale, most cultures can be placed along a scale showing their ranking on this particular dimension: some are high while others are low (See the Fig 2.4 below).

7 In high-context cultures, people are very **homogeneous** regarding experiences, information networks, and the like. Meaning is not necessarily contained in words. In high-context cultures, information is provided through

High-context Cultures
Japanese
Chinese
Korean
African American
Native American
Arab
Greek
Latin
Italian
English
French
American
Scandinavian
German
German-Swiss
Low-context Cultures

Fig 2.4 Cultures Arranged Along the High-context and Low-context Dimension

gestures, the use of space, and even silence. Meaning is also conveyed through status (age, gender, education, family background, title, and affiliations) and through an individual's informal friends and associates. For instance, statements of affection, such as "I love you", are rare because the message is conveyed by the context.

8 In low-context cultures, the population is less. And this lack of a large pool of common experiences means that members of low-context cultures expect messages to be detailed, clear-cut, and definite. If there are not enough data, or if the point being made is not apparent, members of these cultures will ask very **blunt**, even **curt** questions. They feel uncomfortable with the vagueness and ambiguity associated with limited data.

9 This characteristic manifests itself in many ways. For example, the Asian mode of communication is often indirect and implicit, whereas Western communication tends to be direct and explicit. Another problem is that people in high-context cultures perceive low-context people, who rely primarily on verbal messages for information, as less credible. They believe that silence often sends a better message than words, as the Indonesian proverb states, "Empty cans clatter the loudest."

(Adapted from L. A. Samovar et al., *Communication between Cultures*, Chapter 3)

inextricably 密不可分地	blunt 直言不讳的
homogeneous 同类的	curt 唐突失礼的

Discussion

Hofstede's Cultural Dimensions

Psychologist Dr. Geert Hofstede published his cultural dimensions model at the end of the 1970s, based on a decade of research. Since then, it's become an internationally recognized standard for understanding cultural differences. He studied people who worked for IBM in more than 50 countries. Initially, he identified four dimensions that could distinguish one culture from another. Later, he added fifth and sixth dimensions, in cooperation with Dr. Michael H. Bond and Dr. Michael Minkov (Fig 2.5). These are:

(1) Power Distance Index (high versus low);

(2) Individualism Versus Collectivism;

(3) Masculinity Versus Femininity;

(4) Uncertainty Avoidance Index (high versus low);

(5) Long-Versus Short-Term Orientation;

(6) Indulgence Versus Restraint.

Fig 2.5 Hofstede's Cultural Dimensions

Based on the cultural dimensions theory, please analyze:

1. The Chinese policy in handling the coronavirus disease (COVID-19).
2. The phenomenon of "进淄赶烤".
3. The Chinese measures in dealing with the aftermaths of a natural disaster such as an earthquake or a flood, etc.
4. "If Descartes had been Japanese, he would have said, 'We think, therefore we are.'"

Suggestions for Further Reading

Unit 3

Verbal Communication

The notion that thought can be perfectly or even adequately expressed in verbal symbol is idiotic.

— *Alfred North Whitehead*

Learning Objectives

At the end of this unit, you should be able to:

- understand verbal intercultural communication styles;
- identify the difference between Chinese and Western ways of addressing, compliments, apologies and responses;
- learn to achieve equivalence in translation;
- know the influence of pragmalinguistic failures on intercultural communication.

Warm-up Activities

1 Case Study

A Turkish male graduate student in the United States lived in a residence hall where he shared a room with an American. One day his roommate went into the bathroom and completely shaved his head. The Turkish student discovered this fact when he visited the bathroom and saw the hair everywhere. He returned to his room and said to his roommate...

If you were the Turkish student, what would you say to your roommate?

____

The Turkish student said to his roommate, "You've shaved your head?" The American replied,"Yeah, I have."

What did the Turkish student mean by saying "You've shaved your head?"?

____

The Turkish student waited a little, and then said, "I discovered you'd shaved your head when I went into the bathroom and saw the hair." "Yeah," the American confirmed.

What did the Turkish student expect from the American?

____

The Turk was at a loss. He believed he had communicated in the strongest possible language his wish that the American would clean up the mess he'd made in the bathroom.

What's wrong in the communication between the Turk and the American?

____

Questions:

What do you think of the conversation between the Turkish student and the American roommate? Was it a failure or a success? Why?

2 Proverbs and Idioms

Match the Chinese proverbs or idioms in Column A with its equivalent English version in Column B.

Column A

(1) 良言如同蜂房，使心觉得甘甜，使骨得医治。

(2) 一句话说得合宜就如金苹果放在银盘里。

(3) 每个人都是一本好书，只要你懂得如何去阅读他。
(4) 话比剑更能给人以沉重打击。
(5) 学问在成功时是装饰品，在失意时是庇护所，在年老时是营养品。

Column B

a. Every man is a volume if you know how to read him.
b. A word fitly spoken is like apples of gold in the setting of silver.
c. A blow with a word strikes deeper than a blow with a sword.
d. Learning is an ornament in prosperity, a refuge in adversity, and a provision in old age.
e. Pleasant words are a honeycomb, sweet to the soul, and heading to the bones.

Text A

Verbal Intercultural Communication Styles

1 What is verbal intercultural communication?

2 Verbal intercultural communication happens when people from different cultural backgrounds communicate with each other by using language. Language and culture are **inextricably** linked with each other, as known, it is assumed that we can communicate successfully as long as we master the language **proficiently**. However, it is not the case. Successful communication not only depends on what is said but also on how it is said. Culture, **omnipresent** as it is, influences communication at a great level, and different cultures may **render** different communication styles.

3 **Verbal intercultural communication styles**

4 Recognizing the differences in communication styles can help us understand the cultural differences **underpinning** the verbal communication process so as to avoid intercultural communication failures.The different intercultural communication styles are classified into the following five categories: direct and indirect styles; **self-enhancement** and **self-effacement** styles; elaborate, exacting and succinct styles; personal and contextual styles; instrumental and affective styles.

5 **1. Direct and indirect styles**

6 A direct communication style is one in which the speaker's needs, wants, desires, and intentions are **explicitly** communicated. Conversely, an indirect communication style is one in which the speaker's true intentions or needs are only implied or hinted during the conversation.

7 Research indicates that the indirect style is more likely to be used in collectivist cultures, such as in Japan, China and Republic of Korea. The indirect communication style is also more

likely to be used in *high-context cultures*, where meaning is communicated through context rather than explicitly conveyed in words. By comparison, western cultures generally prefer a direct communication style.

8 **2. Self-enhancement and self-effacement styles**

9 The self-enhancement verbal style emphasizes the importance of **boasting** about one's accomplishments and abilities. The self-effacement verbal style, on the other hand, emphasizes the importance of humbling oneself via verbal restraints, hesitations and modest talk, and the use of **self-deprecation** concerning one's achievement.

10 For example, in many Asian cultures, self-effacement talk is expected to signal modesty or humility. In China when someone praises one's child for his or her achievement, verbal self-deprecation is expected, like "That's not worth mentioning", "Don't praise him, he is nothing special" and "It's far from success". When one offers another person a meal that one has prepared, the hostess who apologizes to her guests that "There is nothing special to offer you" has probably "spent two days planning and preparing the meal". Of course the guest should protest such "**disclaimer**" and reemphasize his or her gratitude.

11 In American culture, people encourage individuals to "sell and boast about themselves". Mothers tell their children they are special and unique in the world.

12 **3. Elaborate, exacting and succinct styles**

13 The elaborate style involves the use of rich, expressive and **embellished** language in everyday communication. It can be seen in many Arab, Middle Eastern, and Afro-American cultures, which tend to use metaphorical expressions in every day conversation. For example, rather than simply saying that someone is slender, a comment such as "She is so slim that she can walk between rain drops without getting wet" embellishes and colours the statement.

14 An exacting style, where people focus on **precision** and use of right number of words to convey message, i.e., saying no more or less than is needed, is used by Americans. A **succinct** style is characterized by the use of simple assertions, concise statements, understatements, and even silence. A succinct style can be found in Japan, China, and some Native American cultures.

15 The elaborate style tends to characterize low-context cultures. Conversely, in high-context culture, silence rather than talk can be used to maintain control in a social situation.

16 **4. Personal and contextual styles**

17 The personal style **amplifies** the individual identity of the speaker. It relies on the use of pronouns in sentence construction. For example, English has only one form for the second person, *you*.This style tends to be informal and is often used in individualistic cultures, which emphasize individual goals over those of the group.

18 Contextual communication style, on the other hand, is oriented by status and role. Formality and *power distance* are often emphasized. Contextual style is often seen in collectivistic cultures where one's role identity and status are highlighted. For example, instead of using "you" for all persons, as is the case in

English, in Chinese, German and French exist **elaborated** systems of linguistic forms used to communicate respect to people of different ranks or social status, like 你 and 您, *du* and *Sie*, *tu* and *vous*.

19 **5. Instrumental and affective styles**

20 An instrumental verbal style is sender-based and goal-outcome based, i.e., the instrumental speaker employs communication to achieve some goal or outcome.Instrumental messages often are constructed to persuade and influence others and to maintain one's face.The burden of understanding often rests with the speaker. The speaker carefully chooses and organizes his or her messages in order to be understood by the listener.

21 An affective communication style is receiver and process oriented.The affective speaker is concerned not so much with the outcome of the communication, but with the process.The responsibility of understanding rests with both the speaker and the listener. Affective speakers carefully watch for the reactions of their listener.

inextricably	密不可分地	self-deprecation	自我贬低
proficiently	熟练地	disclaimer	免责声明
omnipresent	无处不在的	embellish	装饰，美化，润饰，布置，对……加以渲染（或发挥）
render	表达，表现；使成为，使变得	precision	精确，准确，细致
underpin	加强，巩固	succinct	简明的，言简意赅的
self-enhancement	自我增强	amplify	放大，增强
self-effacement	谦逊	elaborated	复杂的，详尽的
explicitly	明确地	instrumental	工具性的
boast	自吹自擂	affective	情感性的

Short-answer Questions

Please answer the following questions according to what you've learned from the video clip.

1. Are Chinese always more indirect than Americans? If not, can you give some counter examples?
2. Which verbal communication style impresses you the most? Why? Please provide stories out of your own experience to illustrate.
3. Which verbal style do you think is preferable in contemporary Chinese society, self-enhancement or self-effacement?
4. What verbal communications styles are depicted in this video clip?

SCAN ME!

Reading Comprehension

Each of the following statements contains information in Text A. Decide whether the statement is true (T) or false (F) based on the text.

1. Verbal intercultural communication happens when people from different cultural backgrounds communicate with each other by using language.
2. The direct communication style is also more likely to be used in high-context cultures, where meaning is communicated through context.
3. The self-enhancement verbal style emphasizes the importance of humbling oneself via verbal restraints, hesitations and modest talk.
4. The elaborate verbal communication style tends to characterize high-context cultures.
5. Contextual communication style emphasizes formality and power distance, and is often seen in collectivistic cultures.

Text B

Addressing, Compliments, Apologies and Responses

1 Before you start reading, please look at the following dialogues first.

2 Dialogue 1

3 A: Teacher Zhang, could you come over to our farewell party this Saturday?

4 B: I'd love to. What time?

5 Dialogue 2

6 A: Manager Smith, could I schedule your presentation on our new design for Friday morning?

7 B: I am afraid not. I have something important to do on that morning .

8 Dialogue 3

9 A: Uncle Policeman, could you tell me the way to the railway station?

10 B: Walk down this road and turn left at the second crossing.

11 The above **utterances** are not uncommon for Chinese-English learners. These learners use English to address people in the Chinese way. For Chinese listeners, they are understandable and acceptable, but to foreigners, they sound quite awkward and uncomfortable. Therefore, it is necessary to note some differences between Chinese and English when it comes to addressing people.

12 **Addressing**

13 First, while both Chinese and English people have surnames (last name) and given names (first name or middle names), the order of these names and their use in the two languages differ from each other. In Chinese,

the surname comes first, followed by the given names; but in English this order is reversed.

14 Secondly, many English-speaking people tend to address others by using the first name rather than calling a person Mr. Jack, Mrs. Susie or Miss Juliet, etc. This is especially common among Americans, even when meeting people for the first time. This applies to people of probably all ages, as it is not a sign of disrespect in American culture. Very often it is by no means rude for a child to call a much older person Micheal, Tom or Helen, etc.

15 The Chinese and English customs of addressing family members, relatives and neighbors also differ. In Chinese, "二姐，三哥，四叔，王大伯，张姨，李婶，老李，李老", etc. are respectful forms of addressing, which fit in perfectly with the Confucian idea that the young should respect the old. In English, however, the name alone will generally be enough, with exceptions to addressing one's parents, grandparents, and sometimes an older relative, e.g., Aunt Lily or Uncle Frank. Americans tend to use just the given name, leaving out the term of relationship. Therefore, an American girl simply calls her brother-in-law's mother Susan instead of Auntie Susan.

16 Thirdly, Chinese prefer to address others by using their titles or occupations, such as "李局长，宋经理，刘老师", in which the surname appears before the titles or occupations to show respect for the person concerned. However, this practice is not applicable in English since only a small number of occupations or titles are used before a person's last name: Mr. for a man (teacher, businessman, etc.); Miss for an unmarried woman (teacher, business woman, etc.); Mrs. for a married woman (teacher, director, etc.); Ms. for an unmarried or married woman (teacher, housewife, professional, etc.); Dr. is used to address medical doctors and university professors who have earned a doctorate degree (PhD); Judge for those **authorized** to try cases in a law court; and Governor and Mayor for those who hold such offices, although often used without the surname.

17 Teacher Zhang and Manager Smith mentioned at the beginning are not idiomatic usage of English and therefore sound odd to native speakers.

The following table can be taken as a principle (Table 3.1).

18 The final difference in addressing people rests with the ways of getting attention from a stranger, or a person whose name we may not know. The Chinese like to do so by using a general term such as "同志" (comrade), "师傅" (master) or referring to the stranger as a family member or using a kinship term, such as "大哥" (big brother), "姐姐" (sister), "叔

Table 3.1 Chinese and English Principles of Addressing People

Relationship/Situation	Chinese	English
Formal Relationship/Situation	Surname +Title	Title+Surname
Neutral Relationship/Situation	Surname+Title	Title +Surname/ Given Name
Close Relationship/Informal Situation	Given Name	Given Name

叔"(uncle), partially because speakers, in this way, wish to show their respect for the recipients, gain their favor and establish a harmonious relationship. In contrast, such expressions as "Excuse me","Pardon me" are adopted to attract people's attention in English. Often, people resort to such behaviors as clearing their throat loudly, making some noise or producing meaningful gestures.

19 **Compliments**

20 Before getting into details, please try to find out: How will Chinese and American respond to the following compliments respectively (Table 3.2)?

21 Compliments are an expression of praise, respect, or approval. Appropriate compliments can serve as effective supplementary means in inter-personal communication. Western and Chinese cultures are at polar opposites about complimenting.

22 A Western hostess, if complimented for her cooking skill, is likely to say, "Oh, I am so glad that you like it. I cook it especially for you." Not so is a Chinese hostess, who will instead apologize for giving you "Nothing". They will say: "随便做几个菜，不好吃。" If this is translated into English literally as "I just made some dishes casually and they are not very tasty", perhaps the foreigner will think, "Why do you invite me to your family and have the tasteless food? You are not respecting me."

23 Still bigger differences exist in people's attitude towards compliments. Chinese are tending to **efface** themselves in words or refuse it, although they do feel comfortable about the compliments. So many westerners simply feel puzzled or even upset when their Chinese friends refused their compliments.

24 **Apologies**

25 To offer apologies, both western and Chinese people may say "I am sorry ...", "I apologize for ...", etc. But the Chinese would like to apologize for the crowded state of their dwelling and for small numbers of dishes, even if the room is big enough and there are many dishes. The Chinese say these to express self-depreciation only out of courtesy. But the westerners would wonder: "Since the room is so large and there are so many dishes, why do

Table 3.2 Chinese and English Responses to Different Compliments

Compliments	Chinese Response	English Response
① This is really a nice sweater.		
② You did a good job.		
③ I like your scarf. It's very pretty.		
④ Your English is great!		

they say so? Maybe they do not welcome our visit. They don't like us to eat more." When the Chinese contact with westerners, if they do not know these differences, it will lead to misunderstanding.

26 The ways responding to apologies are different, too.

27 A: Oh, I'm sorry. I forget it.

28 B1: It doesn't matter.

29 B2: That's all right.

30 In the above conversation, B2 is from a westerner, whereas B1 is from a Chinese. "It doesn't matter" is a literal translation of " 没关系 " from Chinese, which is a common pattern in Chinese to respond to apologies. If a Chinese uses this to respond to apologies, westerners will think that he is a sharp person, who simply cannot forgive a very little wrong thing.

utterance	话语，言论	compliment	恭维，称赞
authorize	授权，批准	efface	抹去，消除

Expanded Materials

Reading Comprehension

Which of the following statements can describe the differences between Chinese and English when it comes to verbal intercultural communication as mentioned in Text B? Tick all you can find.

- □ The way people address others.
- □ The way people brag about themselves.
- □ The way people compliment others.
- □ The way people respond to others' praise.
- □ The way people greet each other.
- □ The occasions on which people say "thank you" to others.
- □ The way people prefer to be addressed.
- □ The way people respond to others' apologies.
- □ The way people offer help to others.
- □ The way people make an apology.

Banked Cloze

Fill in the blanks by selecting suitable words from the word bank. You may not use any of the words more than once.

A. attributed	B. restrained	C. responding	D. treated	E. appreciated
F. perceived	G. modesty	H. attempts	I. employ	J. contributing

Language teaching and learning would affect the way of [1] ____________ to compliments. A learner tends to [2] ____________ the responses of the language he or she is learning. For example, if an English learner comes across with a compliment of "Your English is excellent", he or she is more likely to respond with "Thank you", and for an American learner of Chinese, if his or her Chinese is complimented, he or she would react with "哪里，哪里". But when the Chinese learner of English receives Chinese compliments, he tends to react in the typical Chinese way. So is the American learner of Chinese.

Many [3] ____________ have been made to explain the factors [4] ____________ to the differences of compliment strategy between Chinese and American English. It is clear that the compliment, like any other speech act, reflects a variety of cultural norms and values and it serves to express and maintain these values. Compliments in Chinese and American English should not be the exception. Firstly, in Chinese culture, [5] ____________ is always regarded as one of the most important virtues. Denigrating (贬低) others while elevating self is widely [6] ____________ as being "arrogant" or "boasting", therefore, it should be avoided. In American English, individualism and the value of mutual respect and acknowledgement are highly valued. Therefore, for a particular compliment, an acceptance is preferred over a denial as people tend to believe, respect and acknowledge others and choose to be [7] ____________ in the same manner in social interactions.

Secondly, different topics appropriate for complimenting in Chinese and American English are [8] ____________ to different values in Chinese and American cultures. While the appearance of females in Chinese can be complimented, it is not as widely as that in American context. Rather it is sex sensitive and [9] ____________.

Thirdly, the relationship of the speaker and the hearer is another important point when a compliment is used. In American society, equality is highly valued and achievements are greatly [10] ____________. In Chinese society, however, complimenting is sometimes taken as flattery.

Discussion

Do you think there has been some change in the way Chinese respond to compliments in the last decade or two? Why do you think there is such a change?

Text C

Achieving Equivalence in Translation

1 The translation of one language into another is far more complex than most people believe. People tend to assume that text in one language can be accurately translated into another so long as the translator employs a good **bilingual** dictionary. Thanks to the development in technology, artificial intelligence (AI) and GPT, together with many translation Apps and softwares emerged, which in many people's eyes, could make translation done automatically at one touch in real time.

2 Unfortunately, languages are not so simple because (1) words have more than one meaning; (2) many words are culture-bound and have no direct translations; (3) cultural orientations can render a direct translation into **nonsensical**; and (4) a culture may not have the background and understanding to translate experiences specific to other cultures. Therefore, problems often arise in translation when we hope to achieve **equivalence** between languages, including lexical, idiomatic, grammatical-syntactical, experiential, conceptual and functional equivalence.

3 **Lexical equivalence**

4 One of the goals of translation is to convey the meaning of the source language, but dictionary translations rarely reflect common language usage in a culture. Translators also need to deal with **nuances** and with words that have no **equivalents** in other language. Eskimo languages, for example, have many different words to refer to snow. Were you to translate on a word-for-word basis, you would translate all those different words into one English word "snow". Much of the meaning of the more specific and more descriptive words, for example, qualities of **slushiness** or hardness or newness, would be lost in translation. Consider the following as well: does "*Yellow Pages*" mean the same thing as many people might take for granted? A closer look at "风水"(*fengshui*), "磕头""叩头"(*kowtow*), " 饺子 "(*jiaozi*), and "豆腐" (*doufu*) can also illustrate this point.

5 **Idiomatic equivalence**

6 Idiomatic expressions are culture-bound; they do not translate well. Take the example of an Italian idiom translated into English: "Giovanni stamemandoil cane per I'aia." Translated literally, this is: "John is leading his dog around the threshing floor." A better translation, with greater correspondence of meaning, is: "John is beating around the bush." Coming up with the second translation thus requires that the translator be familiar with American idioms. This is one of the reasons why foreign languages are difficult for non-native people to learn. It is easy to think of many idioms in common use in English that can be misunderstood. How do you translate the following phrases?

1. break a leg ____________________
2. pull one's leg ____________________
3. eat one's words ________________
4. hold one's tongue _______________
5. hold one's horses _______________
6. kick the bucket _________________
7. child's play ____________________
8. raining cats and dogs ____________

7 **Grammatical-syntactical equivalence**

8 Difficulties may also arise when there are no **equivalent** grammatical or syntactical features. In the Filipino language, there is no equivalent of the English verb "to be". No relative pronouns in Korean are **comparable** to the English "who", "which", "that", or "what". In Japanese, there is no parallel for the distinctions made in English between modifiers of nouns that are "countable", such as days, teachers, or flavors, and modifiers of nouns that are "uncountable" such as sugar, advice, or communication. As a result, Japanese translations may render statements like "much shoes" or "many patience" .

9 Try to translate the following pairs into Chinese to better understand the syntactical feature of language:

1. plan a table ________________
   table a plan ________________
2. book a place ________________
   place a book ________________
3. lift a thumb ________________
   thumb a lift ________________

10 **Experiential equivalence**

11 If an object or experience does not exist in one culture, it is hard to translate words referring to it into the language of that culture when no word may exist for them. The meanings that cultures have for words are based on shared experiences. When we lack experiential equivalents, we lack the words in our vocabulary to represent those experiences. Take the example — When the vocabulary of a **tribe** in a mountainous jungle region has words for rivers and streams but not oceans, how do you translate the notion of an ocean?More examples in Chinese and English are " 梅雨，清明，三伏，三九，民办教师 ", and *A Midsummer Night's Dream, Ode to the West Wind, Shall I Compare Thee to a Summer's Day*, etc.

12 **Conceptual equivalence**

13 Abstract concepts may not exist in the same fashion in different languages. For example, people in the United States have unique meaning for the word freedom, that meaning is not universally shared. Speakers of other languages may say they are free and are correct in their culture, but the *freedom* they refer to is not equivalent to what people experience as *freedom* in the United States.

14 Difficulty in translation lies in matching concepts. Some concepts are culture-specific and others culture-general. By definition, it is impossible to translate perfectly a culture-specific concept. Strong affection is expressed in English with the verb *to love*. In Spanish, there are two verbs, *teamo* and *tequiero*. *Teamo refers* to **nurturing** love, as between a parent and a child or between two adults. *Tequiero* translates literally as *I want you*, which connotes ownership, a concept not present in the English expression *I love you*. Commonly used to express love between two adults, *tequiero* falls somewhere between the English

statements *I love you* and *I like you*.

15 Functional equivalence

16 Regarding translation problems related to cultural differences, the concept of "functional equivalence" first proposed by **Eugene A. Nida**, provides a guiding principle. It emphasizes that the equivalence of cultural elements overweighs that of words. The "faithfulness" of a translation lies in whether cultural connotations from the source language have been successfully conveyed to the target language.

Eugene A. Nida

(1914-2011)

American linguist, translation theorist;

Ph. D. in linguistics from the University of Michigan in 1943;

Developer of the dynamic-equivalence *Bible* translation theory.

(Adapted from L.A. Samovar et al., *Communication between Cultures*, Chapter 5)

bilingual 双语的	equivalent 对等的
nonsensical 荒谬的，无意义的	comparable 类似的
equivalence 对等	tribe 部落
nuances 细微差别	nurturing 培养，培育
equivalents 对应词	functional equivalence 功能对等
slushiness 融雪，雪泥	Eugene A. Nida 尤金・A. 奈达（1914—2011，美国语言学家、翻译家）

Short-answer Questions

Please answer the following questions according to what you've learned from the textbook.

1. What problems in translation do you think are more difficult to deal with than others? Can you find examples in translation between Chinese and English to illustrate the problem in achieving the above-mentioned six types of equivalence?
2. Why are direct translations difficult in some cases? What can we do about it?

Discussion

Appreciate the film *Lost in Translation* (2003) and figure out the difficulties and functions of translation. How to understand the word "translation" in the title?

Suggestions for Further Reading

Unit 4

Nonverbal Communication

There's language in her eye, her cheek, her lip.

— William Shakespeare

Learning Objectives

At the end of this unit, you should be able to:

- understand the significance of nonverbal communication;
- know about the definition and functions of nonverbal communication;
- identify different categories of nonverbal communication;
- cultivate some skills to communicate nonverbally in a positive manner;
- learn useful words and expressions related to nonverbal communication.

Warm-up Activities

Case Study

Xiao Li, a volunteer Chinese teacher, was assigned to teach in a primary school in Sri Lanka(斯里兰卡). During his very first Chinese class, he was both excited and nervous. After explaining a Chinese grammar point, he asked the students, in Chinese, "你们明白了吗？"(*Nǐmen míngbai le ma? meaning "Do you understand?" in English*). Some nodded, while others shook their heads. So he repeated the explanation, and then asked the students again, "你们明白了吗？" This time, all the students shook their heads. As Xiao Li couldn't understand Sinhala (僧伽罗语), he could only judge whether they understood or not through the students' body language. When he saw the whole class shaking their heads, he couldn't help but explain it one more time, and the students just followed along mechanically. The class went on like this, and at the end of the class, he inquired the students, "你们明白了吗？" The students still shook their heads.

Xiao Li felt sad and extremely exhausted emotionally. He even began to doubt his own competence of being a volunteer Chinese teacher.

> ***Questions:***
> What do you think of Xiao Li's first Chinese class in Sri Lanka? Was it a failure? Why?

Text A

Encountering Nonverbal Communication

1 **What Is Nonverbal Communication?**

2 There is no shortage of definitions for nonverbal communication. We shall select some versions representative, as follows:

3 Nonverbal communication involves *all nonverbal* **stimuli** *in a communication setting that are generated by both the source and his or her use of the environment and that have potential message value for the source or receiver.*

4 Nonverbal communication is *"all those messages that people exchange beyond the words themselves."*

5 Simply put, nonverbal communication is communication without the use of words.

6 **Mehrabian's Rule**

7 Dr. **Albert Mehrabian**, Professor Emeritus of psychology at the University of California, Los

Angeles (UCLA), is known for this research in the role of nonverbal communication, indicating that spoken words (verbal communication) only account for 7% of what a listener perceives; the remaining 93% of the message in communication is conveyed nonverbally — 38% through tone of voice and 55% through facial expressions (body language).This rule is often known as Mehrabian's Rule, as illustrated in the following pie chart (Fig 4.1).

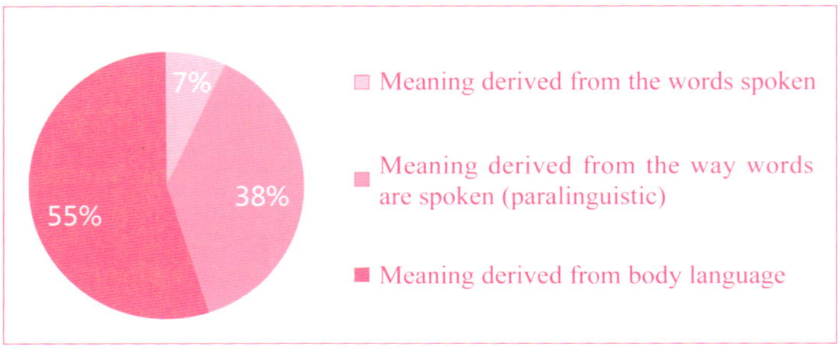

Fig 4.1 Mehrabian's Rule

8 **Why Nonverbal Communication?**

9 Nonverbal communication is important because people make judgments and decisions concerning the internal states of others consciously and unconsciously, intentionally and unintentionally. For example, from tone of voice, to the distance between us and our partners, to the amount of touching in which we engage, we can gather clues to the closeness of our relationships.

10 Nonverbal communication is essential because we use the actions of others to learn about their **affective** or emotional states. If we see someone with a **clenched** fist and a **grim** expression, we know that this person is not happy. If we hear someone's voice **quaver** and see his or her hands tremble, we infer that the person is fearful or anxious.

11 Nonverbal communication is significant because it is usually responsible for first impressions. Think for a moment of how often your first judgments are based on the color of a person's skin or the manner in which he or she is dressed. More importantly, those initial messages usually influence the perception of everything else that follows. Even how we select friends and partners **is grounded in** first impressions.

12 Nonverbal communication has value in human interaction because many of our nonverbal actions are not easily controlled consciously. This means that they are relatively free of **distortions** and **deception**. For example, it is difficult to control a blushing face when we are embarrassed or a clenched jaw when we are angry.

13 Finally, nonverbal communication is important to the study of intercultural communication because a great deal of nonverbal behavior speaks a universal language.Whether in New York, America, or Tianjin, China, people tend to have similar meanings for behaviors such as smiling, frowning, laughing, and crying.

stimuli 刺激（stimulus 的复数）	quaver 颤抖
Albert Mehrabian 艾伯特·麦拉宾（美国心理学家）	be grounded in 以……为基础，以……为根据
affective 情感的，感情的	distortion 变形，扭曲，曲解
clenched 握紧	deception 欺骗
grim 严峻的	

Short-answer Questions

Please answer the following questions according to what you've learned from the textbook.

1. Why is nonverbal communication so important to us?
2. Define nonverbal communication in your own words and provide examples to illustrate your definition.

Reading Comprehension

Each of the following statements contains information in Text A. Decide whether the statement is true (T) or false (F) based on the text.

1. Nonverbal communication is the process of communication through body language.
2. Body language is a kind of nonverbal behavior which can transmit information through gestures, actions, and facial expressions.
3. People in all cultures use nonverbal gestures to communicate consciously.
4. Nonverbal signals can reveal a person's attitude, outlook, interests, and so on.
5. According to Dr. Mehrabian, 7% of a message is conveyed verbally, through words. The other 93% is split between tone of voice (55%) and body language (38%).

Text B

Characteristics & Functions of Nonverbal Communication

1 **1. Characteristics of Nonverbal Communication**

2 (1) *Structured, linguistic and clear vs. unstructured, nonlinguistic and ambiguous*

3 Verbal communication is structured and follows strict rules, while nonverbal communication is unstructured and flexible. The former

depends on the use of language, while the latter does not. Nonverbal communication is non-linguistic; verbal communication is much clearer with the assistance of grammar and vocabulary. But a gesture may be understood in different ways.

4 (2) *Conscious vs. unconscious*

5 Nonverbal behavior is, by and large, unconscious, so it becomes quite difficult to seek clarification of a misunderstood nonverbal cue. Although we can ask someone to repeat a sentence, it is unlikely that we ask someone to explain what he or she meant by a half-smile, a particular posture, or a sudden movement of the head.

6 (3) *Discontinuous vs. continuous*

7 In verbal communication, you take turns in talking, whereas nonverbal communication can go on all the time. For example, when you wear a special dress, it conveys a message, which is there all the time.

8 (4) *Acquired and controllable vs. natural and uncontrollable*

9 Verbal communication is acquired, i.e., it is learned, while much nonverbal communication is in-born. That is, biological forces govern many of our nonverbal actions. For example, you do not have to learn how to smile.

10 (5) *Nonverbal communication is more universal than verbal communication*

11 People who do not understand each other verbally can use gestures to express themselves sometimes. Whether in the United States, China, Australia, or South Africa, people tend to have similar meanings for such behaviors as smiling, waving, frowning, laughing and crying.

12 (6) *Nonverbal messages can be more emotional in their appeal and impact than verbal ones*

13 Physical contact places another layer of meaning on what is being said, and this layer is generally more emotional and forceful than verbal means. For example, your tears, even when perceived by someone from another culture, have a much stronger impact than the words "I am sad".

14 **2. Functions of Nonverbal Communication**

Nonverbal behavior has many uses and unique functions in communication.

15 (1) *Repeating*

People often use nonverbal messages to repeat a point they are trying to make. We might hold up our hand in the gesture that signifies a person to stop at the same time we actually say the word "stop". Or we might point in a certain direction after we have just said, "The new library is south of that lake."

16 (2) *Complementing*

17 You can tell someone that you are pleased with his or her performance, but this message takes on extra meaning if you pat the person on the shoulder at the same time. This behavior is seen to be **accenting** the idea the speaker is making. An apology becomes more forceful if your face, as well as your words, is saying, "I'm sorry."

18 (3) *Substituting*

19 As shown above, the policeman does not need to speak when regulating traffic. If you

see a very special friend, you enlarge the size of your smile and throw open your arms to greet him or her, which is a substitute for all the words it would take to convey the same feeling. If a group of people is **boisterous**, you place your index finger to your lips as an alternative to saying, "Please calm down so that I can speak."

20 (4) *Regulating*

21 We often regulate communication by using some form of nonverbal behavior: we nod our head in agreement to indicate to our communication partner that we agree and that he or she should continue talking; or we remain silent for a moment and let the silence send the message that we are ready to begin our speech.

22 (5) *Contradicting*

23 On some occasions, our nonverbal actions send signals opposite from the literal meanings in our verbal messages. For example, you tell someone you are relaxed, yet your voice **quavers** and your hands shake. Because people rely mostly on nonverbal messages when they receive conflicting data, we need to be aware of the dangers **inherent** in sending opposing messages.

(Adapted from L. A. Samovar et al., *Communication between Cultures,* Chapter 6)

accent	强调	quaver	颤抖，哆嗦
boisterous	喧闹的	inherent	内在的，固有的

Reading Comprehension

Which of the following can describe the characteristics of nonverbal communication as mentioned in Text B? Tick all you can find.

- ☐ Structured, linguistic and clear.
- ☐ Unconscious.
- ☐ Discontinuous.
- ☐ Acquired and controllable.
- ☐ Universal.
- ☐ Natural and uncontrollable.
- ☐ Emotional in appeal and impact.

- Continuous.
- Conscious.
- Unstructured, nonlinguistic and ambiguous.

Banked Cloze

Fill in the blanks by selecting suitable words from the word bank. You may not use any of the words more than once.

A. indicate	B. context	C. ambiguity	D. dense	E. nonverbally
F. repeatedly	G. frustration	H. summon	I. subtle	J. misunderstanding

Differences in nonverbal communication, or body language, are often 1 ____________ and can be the source of intercultural 2 ____________. During my first few days at the College of Micronesia, the division secretary was on sick leave. When she returned I introduced myself and asked, "Are you feeling better?" She answered "Yes" 3 ____________ by raising and lowering her eyebrows. I interpreted her response to mean "What did you say?". So I repeated the question a little more slowly, and again she raised her brows. I asked the question a third time, receiving the same nonverbal response. Out of 4 ____________, I finally said, "I hope you are feeling better soon." About a week later, when I learned that raised eyebrows mean "Yes", I realized that the secretary must have thought me 5 ____________ for repeatedly asking the same question.

Micronesians use the same shake of the head as Americans as a way to say "No." A frown accompanied by a wave of the hand at chest level is an emphatic "No!" or "Stop it!". Micronesians throw their heads slightly back and to the side to 6 ____________ "over there". Depending on the 7 ____________ of the question, the response could mean a few blocks away or the next island over. The apparent 8 ____________ of that particular response was sometimes confusing. Similarly, if I, as an outsider, were to 9 ____________ a Micronesian by 10 ____________ curling my index finger upward, the gesture would imply that the receiver had the status of an animal. More than a few times, I had to control my impulse to use that common gesture. Nonverbal communication is one of the barriers in intercultural communication.

Discussion

1. Identify the function(s) of nonverbal communication employed in the above article. Besides those mentioned in Text B, can you think of some other functions our nonverbal behavior sometimes serve?

2. Which do you think is more effective in achieving our goals in communication, verbal communication or its nonverbal counterpart? Why?

Text C

Classification of Nonverbal Communication (Ⅰ)

1 Classifications of nonverbal behavior may vary, but most classifications divide nonverbal messages into two categories: those that are produced by the *body* (appearance, movement, facial expressions, eye contact, touch, smell, paralanguage); and those that the individual combines with the *setting* (time, space, color and silence).

2 **Body Behavior**

3 **General Appearance and Attire**

4 In intercultural communication, appearance is important because the standards we apply and the judgments we make are subject to cultural interpretations. In America, people tend to value the appearance of tall, slender women; in Japan, however, **diminutive** females are deemed the most attractive.

5 Attire is also a reflection of a culture's value orientation. For example, Muslim girls usually wear scarves to cover their heads, and "girls are not allowed to participate in swimming classes because of the prohibitions against exposing their bodies". The Spanish also link appearance to rank. So in Spain, it is not uncommon to see people of high status wearing a suit and tie in very hot weather.

6 **Body Movement: Kinesics**

7 The study of how movement communicates is called *kinesics*. In general, kinesic cues are those visible body shifts and movements that can send messages about (1) our *attitude* toward the other person (standing face-to-face with a friend, or leaning forward may show that we are relaxed), (2) our *emotional state* (tapping on the table or playing with coins can mean we are nervous), and (3) our *desire to control our environment* (motioning someone to come closer means we'd like to talk to him or her).

8 **Posture**

Posture and sitting habits offer insight into a culture's deep structure. In some Asian cultures, the bow is much more than a greeting. It signifies the culture's concern with *status* and *rank*. In Japan, for example, low posture is an indicator of respect. The person who occupies the lower status begins the bow, and his or her bow must be deeper than the other person's. The superior determines when the bowing is to end. When the participants are of equal rank, they begin the bow in the same manner and end at the same time.

9 In the United States, where being casual and friendly is valued, people often fall into chairs or **slouch** when they stand. In many countries, such as Germany and Sweden, where lifestyles tend to be more formal, slouching is considered a sign of rudeness and poor manners.

10 **Gestures**

11 Gestures refer to specific body movements that carry meaning. Hands can form shapes that convey many meanings. "I have no idea", "Come here", "I can't hear you" and "It' s OK" can be expressed nonverbally using only hands.

12 The following are a few examples of how gestures communicate. Take the "OK" gesture as an example. In many countries like America, it is **emblematic** of the word OK; in Japan (and Republic of Korea) it signifies "money" (*okane*, おかね，お金，钱); and among Arabs this gesture is usually accompanied by a baring of teeth, and together they indicate extreme hostility. This same gesture is obscene in Mexico and Germany, and to the Tunisian it means "I'll kill you".

13 **Facial Expressions**

14 Facial expressions carry meaning determined by contexts and relationships. For instance, the smile, which is typically an expression of pleasure, has many functions.A woman's smile at a policeman who is about to give her a ticket does not carry the same meaning as the smile she gives to a young child.

15 **Eye Contact**

16 Eye contact serves to show intimacy, attention, and influence. In a conversation too little eye contact may be seen negatively because it conveys lack of interest, inattention, or even mistrust. The relationship between mistrust and lack of eye contact is stated, "Never trust a person who can't look you in the eye."

17 **Touch**

18 Just as our words and gestures are messages carrying our internal thoughts and feelings, touch also conveys messages. The meaning we assign to being touched, and our reasons for touching others, help us gain insight into the communication encounter. Studies on touching have uncovered some interesting insights.

19 **Smell**

20 The study of communication via smell is called **Olfactics**. Smell communicates not only when we are face to face with another person, but even when the other person is not present. Americans represent an example of a culture that tends to be uncomfortable with natural smells. Many other cultures regard natural odors as normal, and most Arabs perceive a person's smell as an extension of the person.

21 **Paralanguage**

22 Paralanguage is the way inflections are used when sending a message verbally. It involves the linguistic elements of speech, that is, *how something is said* and not the actual meaning of the spoken words. It could be a person's tone of voice, speed, volume, pitch, stress, pause, intonation, or **articulation**.

23 Most classifications divide paralanguage into three kinds of vocalizations: (1) vocal characterizers (laughing, crying, yelling, moaning, whining, **belching**, yawning); (2) vocal qualifiers (volume, pitch, rhythm, tempo, resonance, tone); and (3) vocal

segregates ("un-huh", "shh" ,"uh", "oooh", "mmmh", "humm").

24 Culture influences our use of and response to paralanguage. Arabs speak very loudly because loudness for them connotes strength and sincerity, while softness communicates weakness and **deviousness**.The Germans conduct their business with a commanding tone that projects authority and self-confidence. On the other hand, there are cultures that have a totally different view toward loud and firm voices. For Thai people, a loud voice is perceived as being impolite. In Japan, raising one's voice often implies a lack of self-control. A barrier occurs when paralanguage is misunderstood or not applied appropriately.

(Adapted from L. A. Samovar et al., *Communication between Cultures*, Chapter 6)

diminutive 娇小的	articulation 清晰度（发音）
slouch 没精打采地站	belch 打嗝
emblematic 象征的；标志的	deviousness 不光明正大
Olfactics 嗅觉学	

Text D

Classification of Nonverbal Communication (Ⅱ)

1 **Time Matters**

2 Culture plays a substantial role in how you perceive and use time. Benjamin Franklin remarked, "Time is money." The Chinese know the Confucian saying, "Think three times before you act." And a Mexican approach to time is seen in the saying, "Do not today what you can do tomorrow." Consider for a moment how differently each of these cultures perceives time.

3 A culture's conception of time can be examined from three perspectives: (1) informal time; (2) perceptions of past, present, and future; and (3) the monochronic and polychronic classifications.

4 **Informal Time**

5 In most instances rules for informal time, such as **punctuality** and pace, are not **explicitly** taught. These rules usually function below the level of consciousness.

6 Our reaction to punctuality is rooted in our cultural experiences. In the Unites States, people have all learned that the boss can arrive late for a meeting without anyone raising an eyebrow; if the secretary is late, he or she may receive a **reprimand** in the form of a **stern** glance. In Latin America, one is expected to arrive late to appointments as a sign of

respect. And in Africa, people often "show up late for appointments, meetings, and social engagements". However, these two views of **tardiness** would be perceived as rudeness in Germany.

7 We can determine a culture's attitude toward time by examining the pace at which members of that culture perform specific acts and respond to certain events. Americans always seem to be in a hurry. Conveniences — from fast-food restaurants, to one-stop gas stations, to microwave ovens — help Americans get things done quickly. But other cultures see time differently and hence live life at a pace different from that of most people in America. The French, Chinese and Japanese do not share the American sense of urgency to accomplish tasks. The Chinese have a proverb: "He who hurries cannot walk with dignity."

8 **Past, Present and Future**

9 Cultures with a past orientation view the traditions of what came before as being more important in many ways than the present. Japan, India, China, and numerous cultures of Eastern Europe have always placed a significant value on past achievement and on honoring the lives and spirits of ancestors; they resist change. The Chinese and Japanese, with traditions of ancestor worship and strong pride in their cultures' persistence for thousands of years, use the past as a guide to live in the present. As a Chinese proverb advises, "Consider the past and you know the present." Cultures that value the past are more likely to respect and **venerate** the elderly than cultures that value the future.

10 Cultures with a present orientation are focused on the moment, emphasizing enjoying and living in the moment, neither invoking the past nor wondering about the future. Societies with simple patterns of organization, fewer rules and norms, and very little outside influence often exhibit such views. Numerous Pacific Islanders, and the Maoris of New Zealand see time as a seamless continuum that passes over us. They tend to be more impulsive and spontaneous than others and often have a casual, relaxed lifestyle.

11 The third orientation, which puts great faith in the future, is the one most developed nations of the modern, global economy have. Having an eye to the future often produces a very low tolerance for extensions and postponements. In addition, future-oriented cultures welcome innovation and change and "have less regard for past social or organizational customs and traditions".

12 **Monochronic and Polychronic Classifications**

13 The concepts of monochronic and polychronic time come from Edward T. Hall. Monochronic (one dimensional) societies are those that are punctual, efficient, and attach importance to being on time. These are mostly **linear** thinkers who see time as scarce, valuable, something to be saved.

14 Monochronic people feel more comfortable if they are able to stick to the original plans, meet established deadlines, and use their time wisely. In return, they expect others to be prompt, to respect their own use of time, and to adapt quickly to make the most of the time they have been given.

15 Nations with a monochronic view of time are usually among the more individualistic cultures, such as the U.S., Canada, and northern Europe, but other collectivistic cultures, such as Japanese (largely because of global economic development), also fall into this category.

16 In polychronic (multidimensional) societies, people are more relaxed about time because relationships are more important than schedules. Relationships are crucial to developing trust, which evolves through these relationships and ultimately makes for good business. Usually the more collectivistic cultures see time this way, such as cultures from Asia, Latin America, and the Middle East. Other European cultures, such as French, Spanish , and Irish, also fall into this category. In many developing nations, traditional notions of time have come into conflict with more modern, monochronic concepts. Still, nations such as India, Brazil, Mexico, and Vietnam are learning to live with both of these concepts: one time for business (usually with foreigners), and another for the things in life that really matter.

17 In short, monochronic culture is noted for its emphasis on schedules, segmentation and promptness; while polychronic culture is less rigid and less clock-bound. In the chart below, more differences are shown (Table 4.1).

Table 4.1 Monochronic Culture and Polychronic Culture

Monochronic Culture	Polychronic Culture
Preset schedules dominate interpersonal relations.	Interpersonal relations supercede present schedules.
Appointment time is rigid.	Appointment time is flexible.
People handle one task at a time.	People handle many tasks simultaneously.
Time is inflexible and tangible.	Time is flexible and fluid.
Personal time and work time are clearly separated.	Personal time and work time are not clearly separated.
Organizational tasks are measured by activities per hour or minute.	Organizational tasks are measured as part of overall organizational goal.
Austria, Germany, Switzerland, U. S.	Africans, Arabs, Greeks, Mexicans, Portuguese, Spanish, most Asian cultures.

18 Intercultural Lens: Understand the concept of time

19 Suppose you are in America and are invited to a friend's house for dinner at 6: 00 p. m. What time should you arrive?

A. 5: 30 p. m.

B. 6: 00 p. m.

C. 7: 00 p. m.

20 In North America, these are the reactions you might get if you arrived at these times. Why?

21 Space Talks

22 Edward T. Hall once remarked, "Space talks."Unconsciously, we all keep a comfortable distance around us when interacting with other people. This distance has had several names over time, including "personal space", "interpersonal distance", "comfort zone", and "body bubble".

23 The size of your "bubble" depends on your cultural background. The difference in personal space rules can cause misunderstandings and even some discomfort in intercultural interactions.

24 For example, in one university, there were reports of miscommunication between Arab and American students. The Arab students complained that the American students were distant and rude, while the American students characterized the Arab students as pushy, arrogant, and impolite.

25 The problem was that the two groups were operating with different rules of personal space. The Arab students were accustomed to standing closer together when talking, while the American students had been raised to do just the opposite.

26 Dr. Hall proposed "four zones" concerning the space bubble, namely the intimate distance, the personal distance, the social distance, and the public distance. People's shifts in voice are also adjusted with regard to the zones of distances, as shown below (Table 4.2):

Table 4.2 Four Zones Proposed by Edward T. Hall

Zone	Distance	Description	Voice
Intimate 	Touching to 18 inches (0-46 cm)	Private situations with people who are emotionally close (e.g. lovers, couples, family members, etc.). If others invade this space, we feel threatened.	Whisper
Personal 	18 inches to 4 feet (46-120 cm)	The lower end is the "handshake" distance — the distance between friends or most couples who stand in public .	Soft voice
Social 	4 feet to 12 feet (120-360 cm)	The lower end is the distance between salespeople and customers and between people who work together in business .	Full voice
Public 	Greater than 12 feet (greater than 360 cm)	Situations such as teaching in a loud voice in a classroom or delivering a speech.	Loud voice

27 Color: Making Communication More "Colorful"

28 Colors may help make communication in more "colorful". Black is the color of mourning to many Europeans and Americans, but white is worn to funerals in China, Japan and many other nations. In the United States, white is, however, typically worn by brides while in India, red or yellow is worn. Purple is sometimes associated with royalty, but it is the color of death in many Latin American countries. Red (especially red roses) is associated with romance in some cultures. But red is not an appropriate color for wrapping gifts in Japan. Dark red is the color of mourning along the **Ivory Coast**.

29 Green is not used for wrapping packages in Egypt since green is the nationalist color (as are red, white and blue in the United States). Men should avoid wearing a green hat in China as this signifies that their wife betrays them. So in the business setting, presenting a green hat as a gift to the Chinese men may be disastrous. In many countries, blue is considered a masculine color, but to people of France and the United Kingdom, red is more masculine. Blue, in Iran, is an undesirable color. While Americans consider pink to be the most feminine color, people in most other countries think of yellow as the most feminine.

30 Silence: Not Necessarily Silent

31 There is a story of how the American philosopher Ralph Waldo Emerson "talked" in silence for hours to the English writer Thomas Carlyle. It seems that Emerson, on a visit to Europe, arranged to meet with Carlyle, who was his idol. Emerson maintains they sat together for hours in perfect silence until it was time for him to go, then parted cordially, congratulating each other on the fruitful time they had together.

32 Silence is a form of nonverbal communication that may be interpreted in various ways depending upon the situation, the duration of the silence, and the culture. In most American contexts, silence is not highly valued, for it is usually viewed as empty pauses or ignorant lapses. However, in many other cultures, especially the high context cultures, silence may hold the meanings as strong and contextual as language. As the proverb goes, "Speech is silver, silence is golden".

(Adapted from E. T. Hall, *The Silent Language*, Chapter 10; and L. A. Samovar et al., *Communication between Cultures*, Chapter 6)

punctuality	准时；守时	tardiness	迟到；迟延
explicitly	明确地	venerate	崇敬，尊敬
reprimand	训斥；谴责	linear	线性的
stern	严厉的	Ivory Coast	象牙海岸（科特迪瓦（国名）的旧称）

Discussion

A Psychological Quiz on Space:

Where do you prefer in the classroom?

Make your choice.

- [ ] Front
- [ ] Back
- [ ] By window
- [ ] By door
- [ ] Middle

Suggestions for Further Reading

Unit 5

Cross-gender Communication

Men are from Mars. Women are from Venus.

— John Gray

Learning Objectives

At the end of this unit, you should be able to:

- understand "sex" and "gender" in cultural perspective;
- understand the differences between feminine and masculine communication cultures;
- understand the gender differences in communication;
- know how to achieve effective cross-gender communication.

Warm-up Activities

1 Case Study I

Tricky Feedback

Roseanne and Drew are colleagues in a marketing firm. One morning Drew drops into Roseanne's office to discuss an advertising with her. As Drew presents his ideas, Roseanne nods and says "Um", "Uh huh" and "Yes". When he finishes and asks what she thinks, Roseanne says, "I really don' t think that plan will sell the product." Feeling misled, Drew demands, "Then why do you agree the whole time I presented my idea?" Completely confused, Roseanne responds, "What makes you think I was agreeing with you?"

Comment:

Here, the problem arises when Drew translates Roseanne's feedback according to rules of communication in masculine culture. Women learn to give lots of response cues — verbal or nonverbal behaviors — to indicate interest and involvement in the conversation, because that is part of using communication to build relationships with others. Masculine culture, however, focuses on outcomes more than processes, so men tend to use feedback to signal specific agreement or disagreement. When Drew hears Roseanne's "Ums", "Uh huhs", and "Yeses", he assumes she is agreeing. According to feminine culture, however, Roseanne is only showing interest and being responsive, not signaling agreement.

2 Case Study II

Expressing Care

Dedrick and Melita have been dating for two years and are very serious. To celebrate their anniversary, Melita wants to spend a quiet evening in her apartment where they can talk about the relationship and be alone with each other. When Dedrick arrives, he's planned to dine out and go to a concert. Melita feels hurt that he doesn't want to talk and spend the evening alone with her.

Comment:

In feminine culture, talking is a way — probably the primary way — to express and expand closeness. For women, dialog creates a bond. Masculine socialization, in contrast, stresses doing things and shared activities as primary ways to create and express closeness. A man is more likely to express his feelings for a woman by doing something concrete for her (e.g. washing her car and fixing an appliance) or doing something with her (e.g. skiing, going to a concert and playing tennis) than by talking explicitly about feelings. By realizing that actions speak, women can avoid feeling hurt by partners who prefer activities. In addition, women who want to express care in a way that men understand might consider what can be done for or with the men, rather than what to say.

Text A

Sex and Gender

1 What is sex? What is gender? Sex is determined by **genetic** codes that program **biological** features. The words like "man", "woman", "male" and "female" indicate sexual **identities**. Gender is more complex than sex. For example, you might think of gender as the cultural meaning of sex. Since the first cry in this world, individuals are **besieged** with "communications reflecting cultural **prescriptions**" for gender. Gender socialization continues with interactions between parents, teachers, **peers**, and the media. Through our interactions with others, we receive constant messages that reinforce females' **conformity** to **femininity** and males' to masculinity. For instance, parents may say to their daughter who are jumping and laughing too **boisterously**, "Behave like a girl!", while they may tell their crying son, "Be a man. No tears!". This means that individuals are not born with a gender, but are gendered. Although some people **resist** gender socialization, the **intensity** and **pervasiveness** of social prescriptions for gender **ensure** most females will become feminine and most males will become masculine. So gender is a social creation, not an individual characteristic. Everyone is **consciously** or unconsciously gendered the minute he or she comes into the world (Table 5.1).

2 In all, gender and sex are not synonymous. Sex is determined by genetics and biology, while gender is produced and reproduced by society. Societies create meanings of gender; in turn, individuals become gendered as they **embody** social prescriptions in their personal identities (Table 5.2).

Table 5.1 Differences between Sex and Gender

Sex	Gender
biological	socially-constructed
permanent	varied over time and across cultures
with an individual property	with a social and relational quality

Table 5.2 Differences between Girl's and Boy's Interaction

Girl's Interaction (unstructured, cooperative)	Boy's Interaction (more structured, individualized)
Be cooperative, collaborative, and inclusive. It's important that everyone feels involved and has a chance to play.	Assert oneself. Use talk and action to highlight one's ideas and to establish one's status and leadership.
Don't criticize or outdo others. Cultivate egalitarian relationships so the group is cohesive and gratifying to all.	Focus on outcomes. Use talk and actions to make things happen, to solve problems, and to achieve goals.
Pay attention to the feelings and needs of others and be sensitive in responding to them.	Be competitive. Vie for attention. Keep attention focused on you,outdo others, and make oneself stand out.

3 In summary, girls' games occur within a gender culture that emphasizes cooperation, sensitivity toward others, and experience more than outcome. Boy's games emphasize achievement, both for the team and for the individual members. Here interaction is more an arena for negotiating power and status than for building relationships with others.

4 Both **psychodynamic** theories and social science research offer a coherent picture of how gender cultures are produced and what they **entail**. Table 5.3 summarizes the differences between feminine and masculine communication cultures.

Table 5.3 Differences between Feminine and Masculine Communication Cultures

Feminine Talk	Masculine Talk
1. Use talk to build and sustain rapport with others.	1. Use talk to assert yourself and your ideas.
2. Share aspects about yourself and learn about others through disclosure.	2. Avoid personal disclosures that can make you vulnerable.
3. Use talk to create symmetry or equality between people.	3. Use talk to establish your status and power.
4. Matching experiences with others shows understanding and empathy. ("I know how you feel.")	4. Matching experiences is a competitive strategy to command attention. ("I can top that.")
5. To support others by expressing an understanding of their feelings.	5. To support others, do something helpful — give advice or solve a problem for them.
6. Include others in conversation by asking their opinions and encouraging them to elaborate. Waiting one's turn to speak so others can participate.	6. Don't share the talk stage with others. Interrupt others to make your own points.
7. Keep the conversation going by asking questions and showing interest in others' ideas.	7. Each person is on his or her own; it is not your responsibility to help others join in.
8. Be responsive. Let others know you hear and care about what they say.	8. Use responses to make your own points and to outshine others.
9. Be tentative so that others feel free to add their ideas.	9. Be assertive so others perceive you as confident and in command.
10. Talking creates human relationships in which details and interesting comments can enhance the connection.	10. Talking is a linear sequence that should convey information and accomplish goals. Extraneous details get in the way and achieve nothing.

genetic 遗传的	resist 抵抗，反对
biological 生物的	intensity 强度，强烈
identity 身份	pervasiveness 普遍性，广泛性
besiege 围攻，困扰	ensure 确保，保证
prescription 规定，处方	consciously 有意识地
peer 同辈，同行	embody 体现，具体化
conformity 一致性，遵从	psychodynamic 心理动力学的
femininity 女性特质，女性气质	entail 牵涉，需要
boisterously 喧闹地，粗鲁地	

Expanded Materials

Text B

Masculinity and Feminity

1 In addition to the physiological differences between men and women, there are other less obvious gaps lay in the behavior and thinking styles of the two genders.

2 As a female, have you ever complained in private when your boyfriend just tells you to “drink more water” after knowing that you catch a cold?

3 As a male, does it sometimes occur to you that your girlfriend is particularly unreasonable and hard to communicate with?

4 Hofstede uses the words **masculinity** and **femininity** to refer to the degree to which masculine or feminine traits are valued and revealed. His **rationale**, that is supported by most anthropologists, psychologists, and political scientists, is that many masculine and feminine behaviors are learnt and mediated by cultural norms and traditions.

5 Masculinity is the extent to which the dominant values in a society are male oriented and is associated with such behaviors as ambition, differentiated sex roles, achievement, the acquisition of money, and signs of manliness. In a masculine society, men are taught to be domineering and assertive and women nurturing.

6 Hofstede advances an excellent summary of these values when he notes:

7 Masculine cultures use the biological

existence of two sexes to define very different social roles for men and women. They expect men to be **assertive**, **ambitious**, competitive, and to strive for material success, and to respect whatever is big, strong, and fast.

8 Ireland, the Philippines, Greece, Venezuela, Austria, Japan, Italy, and Mexico are among countries where you can find many of the masculine values described by Hofstede. For example, in Japan, despite the high level of economic development, the division of labor finds most men in the role of provider; a woman is a home-maker and breeder.

9 Femininity is the extent to which the dominant values in a society are female oriented and is associated with such behaviors as caring, **nurturing**, interdependence, modesty, and cooperation. Gender roles in feminine societies are more **fluid** than in masculine societies. In a feminine society men need not be assertive and that they can assume nurturing roles. It also promotes sexual equality and holds that people and the environment are important.

10 Cultures that value femininity as a trait stress nurturing behavior. In addition, in feminine cultures there tend to be overlapping social roles for sexes. Interdependence and **androgynous** behavior are the ideal, and people sympathize with the unfortunate. Nations such as Sweden, Norway, Finland, Denmark, and the Netherlands tend toward a feminine world view.

11 Whether or not a culture stresses one trait over another can be seen in a variety of ways. For instance, placing a greater value on masculine over feminine traits can even be seen in the type of person a culture selects to lead it. For example, in Sweden, which had the highest ranking in Hofstede's femininity category, women occupy 41 percent of legislative positions; in Japan, ranked the highest in masculine traits, only 5 percent of legislative offices are held by women.

masculinity	男子气概	ambitious	有雄心的
femininity	女性特质	nurturing	养育的，培育的
rationale	理论依据，理由	fluid	流动的，流畅的
assertive	自信的，断言的	androgynous	雌雄同体的

Text C

Gender Differences in Communication

1 All of us have different styles of communicating with other people. Our style depends on a lot of things: where we are from, how and where we were brought up, what education we received and how old we are. It can also depend on our gender. Generally

speaking, men and women talk differently although there are **varying** degrees of masculine and feminine speech characteristics in each of us. But men and women speak in particular ways mostly because those ways are associated with their gender.

2 The styles that men and women use to communicate have been described as "debate vs. relate", "report vs. rapport" or "competitive vs. cooperative". Men often seek straightforward solutions to problems and useful advice whereas women tend to try and establish intimacy by discussing problems and showing concern and **empathy** in order to reinforce relationships.

3 Jennifer Coates, in her book *Women, Men and Language* (Longman Inc., 1986) studied men-only and women-only discussion groups and found that when women talk to each other they reveal a lot about their private lives. They also stick to one topic for a long time, let all speakers finish their sentences and try to have everyone participate. Men, on the other hand, rarely talk about their personal relationships and feelings but compete to prove themselves better informed about current affairs, travel, sport, etc. The topics change often and the men try to over time establish a reasonably stable **hierarchy**, with some men dominating conversation and others talking very little. Dr. Lillian Glass's book *He Says, She Says, Closing the Communication Gap between the Sexes* (The Putnam Berkeley Group,1993) details her findings on the many differences in the way men and women communicate both verbally and **nonverbally**. You can have a look at the differences as shown in Table 5.4 to Table 5.7.

Table 5.4 Body Language

Men	Women
They take up more physical space when sitting or standing, with arms and legs stretched out away from their bodies.	They take up less physical space, sitting with arms and legs toward their bodies .
They gesture away from the bodies.	They gesture toward the bodies.
They assume more reclined positions when sitting and lean backward when listening.	They assume more forward positions when sitting and lean forward when listening.
They are not as sensitive to the communication cues of others.	They have greater sensitivity and acuity toward other people's nonverbal communication cues.
They tend to approach women more closely in terms of their personal space.	They do not approach men as closely in terms of their personal space.

Table 5.5 Facial Expression

Men	Women
They tend to cock their heads to the side and look at the other person from an angle when listening.	They tend to look at the other person directly facing them with their heads and eyes facing forward when listening.
They provide fewer facial expressions in feedback and fewer reactions.	They provide more facial expressions and more reactions.
They tend to display frowning and squinting when listening.	They display smiling and head-nodding when listening.
They stare more in negative interaction.	They lower their eyes more to avert gaze in negative interaction.

Table 5.6 Speech Pattern

Men	Women
They speak in a louder voice.	They speak in a softer voice.
They use loudness to emphasize points.	They use pitch and inflection to emphasize points.
They sound more monotonous in speech. They use approximately 3 tones when talking.	They sound more emotional in speech. They use approximately 5 tones when talking.
They interrupt others more and allow fewer interruptions.	They interrupt others less and allow more interruptions.
They disclose less personal information about themselves.	They disclose more personal information about themselves.
They make direct accusations (i.e. "You don't call.").	They make more indirect accusations. They use "why", which sounds like nagging (i.e. "Why don't you ever call?").
They make more direct statements and "beat around the bush" less often.	They make more indirect statements .
They make more declarative statements (i.e."It's a nice day.").	They make more tentative statements and use "tag endings" or upward inflections which make statements sound like questions (i.e." It's a nice day , isn't it?").
They use more interjections when changing topics (i.e. "Hey!" "Oh!" "Listen!").	They use more conjunctions when changing topics (i.e. "and", "but", "however").
They ask fewer questions to stimulate conversations.	They ask more questions to stimulate conversations.
They rarely discuss their personal life in business.	They tend to establish more business relationships by discussing their personal life.

Table 5.7 Behavior

Men	Women
They try to solve problems and troubles.	They try to match troubles by relating similar negative experience.
They have a more analytical approach to problems.	They have a more emotional approach to problems.
They are less likely to ask for help. They try to figure things out on their own. They are more task-oriented (i.e."What is everyone going to do?").	They are more likely to ask for help and accept it. They are more maintenance-oriented (i.e. "Is everyone all right?").
They appear less intuitive and less aware of details.	They appear more intuitive and more aware of details.
They have more difficulty in expressing intimate feelings.	They have less difficulty in expressing intimate feelings.
They are more apt to yell, shout and swear to release anger.	They are more apt to cry to release anger.
They talk more about what they did, where they went and less about relationships with others.	They talk more about how they feel and more about relationships with others.
They tend to take verbal rejection less personally.	They tend to take verbal rejection more personally.

vary 变化，不同	hierarchy 等级制度
empathy 同情心，共鸣	nonverbally 非言语地

Expanded Materials

Reading Comprehension

Discuss the following questions with your partner.

1. In what way do men and women communicate differently?
2. How do men differ from women in body language, facial expression, speech pattern and behavior?
3. What is the first and foremost principle for effective cross-gender communication?
4. Can we apply a single criterion to cross-gender communication? Why or why not?
5. How can one enlarge his/her communication style?

Exercises

Complete the following sentences according to the knowledge you have learned.

1. Men enjoy giving information as a way to _______. Women like sharing information to_______.

A. show expertise

B. build relationships

2. Women listen to ________. Men listen to _________.

A. solve problems

B. gain understanding

3. Men tend to make unilateral decisions and are more comfortable giving and taking ________. Women tend to seek input and consensus and are more comfortable with giving and taking _______.

A. suggestions

B. orders

4. Men tend to argue more and find it interesting to ________. Women more often seek ________ and see ________ as more threatening to relationships.

A. disagree

B. disagreement

C. agreement

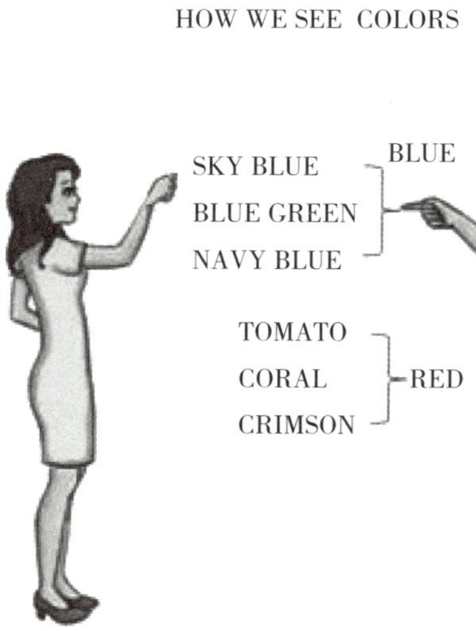

Banked Cloze

Fill in the blanks by selecting suitable words from the word bank. You may not use any of the words more than once.

A. target	B. encourage	C. addressed	D. access	E. sustain
F. positive	G. standards	H. engagement	I. productivity	J. initiative
K. adverse	L. integration	M. undeniable	N. reinforce	O. key

Gender gaps are pervasive in all walks of economic life and imply large losses in terms of foregone [1] ____________ and living [2] ____________ to the individuals concerned and the economy. This report focuses on how best to close these gender gaps under four broad headings: a) Gender equality, social norms and public policies; and gender equality in b) education; c) employment and d) entrepreneurship.

Key policy messages are as follows.

✧ Greater gender equality in educational attainment has a strong [3] __________ effect on economic growth.

✧ Stereotyping needs to be [4] __________ in educational choices at school from a young age. For example, adapt teaching strategies and material to increase [5] __________ of boys in reading and of girls in maths and science; [6] __________ more girls to follow science, engineering and maths courses in higher education and seek employment in these fields.

✧ Good and affordable childcare is a [7] __________ factor for better gender equality in employment. But change also has to happen at home as the bulk of housework and caring is left to women in many countries. Policy can [8] __________ such change, for example, through parental leave policies that explicitly include fathers.

✧ Support policies for women-owned enterprises need to [9] __________ all existing firms, not just start-ups and small enterprises. Equal [10] __________ to finance for male and female entrepreneurs needs to be assured.

Discussion

Have you ever discovered anything intriguing, mysterious or confusing regarding the differences between the two genders?

Suggestions for Further Reading

Unit 6

Culture Diversity and Culture Shock

The gentleman pursues harmony instead of homogeneity; the vulgar man seeks uniformity at the sacrifice of harmony.

— Confucius

Learning Objectives

At the end of this unit, you should be able to:

- learn about the "World Cultural Diversity Promotion";
- understand culture diversity and the differences between the East and West;
- understand what the culture shock is and how to adapt to culture shock;
- understand what the reverse culture shock is and how it happens.

Warm-up Activities

1 Case Study I

Ten years ago, I met a Chinese doctor in the United States, and fell in love with him. In less than 6 months we got married. After my graduation we returned to Finland. My husband had wished to bring his mother to live with us for a while. Last summer, after we redecorated our house, we invited her over. You can well imagine how happy my husband was! And I was just as happy. I know being filial to parents is a great value Chinese people cherish. As a wife of a Chinese, I try to be as filial as my husband. Two days after my mother-in-law' s arrival, I talked to my husband, Dick, while his mother was sitting there.

Dick: What do you mean by asking her?

Litz: I mean what I said. Just ask her how long she' s going to stay.

Can you guess what was going to happen the next day? My mother-in-law overheard our conversation, and decided to leave for China the very afternoon. I had never expected that her visit should be so short. I tried very hard to persuade her to change her mind, but in vain.

Questions:

1. Why did the Chinese mother-in-law decide to leave the very afternoon?
2. What was wrong with Litz asking her husband how long his mother was going to stay after her mother-in-law's arrival?
3. What do you think Litz should do to avoid the misunderstanding between her mother-in-law and her?

2 Case Study II

Steve and Yaser first met in their chemistry class at an American university. Yaser was an international student from Jordan. He was excited to get to know an American. He wanted to learn more about American culture. Yaser hoped that he and Steve would become good friends.

At first, Steve seemed very friendly. He always greeted Yaser warmly before class. Sometimes he offered to study with Yaser. He even invited Yaser to eat lunch with him. But after the semester was over, Steve seemed more distant. The two former classmates didn't see each other very much at school. One day Yaser decided to call Steve. Steve didn't seem very interested in talking to him. Yaser was hurt by Steve's change of attitude. Steve said, "We were friends." Yaser complained, "And I said friends were friends forever."

Questions:

1. What was wrong in the relationship between Yaser and Steve? Who, Yaser or Steve, was to be blamed for it?
2. Do you think it is reasonable for one to conclude from Yaser's experience that Americans are fickle? Why or why not?

3 Case Study III

The director of a Chinese language program at an American university has given two Chinese language teachers from China teaching assignments. During the meeting, neither of the two Chinese teachers raised any objections, but after the meeting, they found the director to propose that their workload was not reasonable and asked for some adjustments. The American director was annoyed. He couldn't understand why they didn't bring it up at the meeting, but expressed dissatisfaction afterwards. He even suspected the character of Chinese teachers. In this regard, the explanation of the two teachers is: they are embarrassed to say it face to face, because they have to take into account the face of another person, afraid of hurting the harmony. But the US director believes that this will have a negative impact on both work and personal relationships.

Questions:

1. What are the problems in the cross-cultural communication experience of these Chinese teachers?
2. How do you explain these cross-cultural misunderstandings or conflicts?
3. What would you do if you were in a similar situation?

Text A

Cultural Diversity

❶ In November 2001, the **UNESCO** adopted the "World Cultural Diversity Promotion".

❷ **Cultural diversity** is very important to the world. Almost three-quarters of the major **conflicts** are cultural related. Development is also inseparable from culture. To improve people's awareness of the importance of cultural diversity, the UNESCO declared May 21st to be the World Day for Cultural Diversity.

❸ Held every year on 21st of May "The Cultural

Diversity for Dialogue and Development" is celebrated all over the world. It highlights not only the richness of the world's cultures, but also the essential role of intercultural dialogue for achieving peace and **sustainable development**.

4 Why does cultural diversity matter?

5 Cultural diversity is a driving force of development. It is also an asset that is important to poverty reduction and sustainable development. **Bridging the gap** between cultures is urgent and necessary for peace, **stability** and development.

6 What should we do?

7 China consistently **highlights** diversity and harmony.

8 While faced with challenges from the West, China takes every chance to clarify its stand from all **perspectives**, including history, culture, diplomacy, military, economy, and so on. Emphasis on harmony rather than **conformity** is repeatedly reinforced. Just as President Xi Jinping has said in his keynote speech delivered at UNESCO headquarters in Paris in 2014, "The Chinese have long come to appreciate the wisdom of 'harmony without uniformity'...We need to encourage different civilizations to respect each other and live together in harmony while promoting their exchanges and mutual learning as a bridge of friendship among peoples, a driving force behind human society, and a strong bond for world peace." This is the Chinese attitude towards the diversity of civilizations, as well as the paths of development of nations. A community with a shared future for mankind is what China is **devoted** to constructing. The peaceful rise of China is an opportunity for the world.

9 Culture is the flower of the human being — the fruit of our minds, the product of our traditions. As a student, firstly, we should learn to respect different cultures, trying to broaden our horizon. Secondly, we should study and understand differences between cultures in order to challenge the prejudice and **foster** mutual respect. Hands in hands, we create a better world with brighter future.

UNESCO	联合国教科文组织	highlight	强调
cultural diversity	文化多样性	perspective	视角，看法
conflict	冲突	conformity	一致性，遵从
sustainable development	可持续发展	devote	奉献，致力于……
bridge the gap	沟通，缩小差距	foster	促进，培养
stability	稳定，稳定性		

Expanded Materials

Expanded Materials

Reading Comprehension

Each of the following statements contains information in Text A. Decide whether the statement is true (T) or false (F) based on the text.

1. The UNWTO declared May 21st to be the World Day for Cultural Diversity.
2. Chinese culture emphasizes on harmony rather than conformity.
3. President Xi Jinping made a keynote speech at the headquarters of UNESCO in Praha in 2014.

Text B

Thinking Patterns in the East and West

1 The ways of thinking is quite different: actually, people live in certain areas have their own way of thinking. It connects to various kinds of factors, such as geography, history, nationality and so on. The ways of thinking are the important reason of cultural difference. It includes knowledge, concepts, methods, language and customs and so on.

2 **Differences in Thinking Patterns in the East and West**

3 Differences in thinking patterns in the East and West can be summarized as the following: Chinese thinking pattern is more likely to be **synthetic**, **intuitive**, and **concrete**, valuing

subjectively and wholeness. While Western thinking pattern is more likely to be analytical, statistical, rational, and **circumspect**, laying more emphasis on objectivity, specificity and precision.

4 **Synthesis vs. Analysis**

5 Generally speaking, the Chinese are synthetically thought-oriented. Synthetic thought inclines to combine separate parts of an object or idea into a unity, and integrates its qualities, relations, and the alike. People with this kind of thinking pattern would strive for unity between events or objects and given signs or symbols. People with synthetic thought regard human and nature, human and **cosmos** order, and individual and society as an inseparable and dependent whole.

6 In contrast with the Chinese, the English-speaking people prefer to think **analytically**. Analytical thought is a process of dividing a whole into concrete details and simpler elements for the study of their characteristics, functions, and relations. It clarifies the differences of subject and object, men and nature, spirits and materials, imagination and existence, soul and flesh, appearance and essence, etc.

7 As a result of analytical thinking, people in the English-speaking countries tend to be good at classification and categorization and thus they prefer making use of concepts for logical judgment and reasoning. As a result of synthetic mode of thinking, Chinese people tend to be good at gaining intuitive insight and thinking in terms of images.

8 The analytical and synthetic differences in thinking patterns between the East and West can be typically reflected in the following examples:

9 Western Medicine and Traditional Chinese Medicine (TCM) (Table 6.1)

Table 6.1 Western Medicine and Traditional Chinese Medicine (TCM)

Western Medicine	Traditional Chinese Medicine (TCM)
It regards the human body as an object that can be studied and controlled.	It regards the human body as a part of nature , bring it back to balance.
It divides the human body into different parts and treats them accordingly.	It looks at the body as an organic whole.
Patients have to go to different departments to get treated.	It considers the connections of different parts of the body.
A lot of tests (analyses) done before decision made.	A patient suffering from headache may get some foot treatment.

10 Painting

11 Chinese painting can be a synthesis of different art forms: **calligraphy**, painting, poetry and stamp. While in the West, painting is painting and poetry is poetry: in Chinese painting, the eyes of the viewer are assumed to move across the surface of the painting, while in the Western painting, there is only one focal point, one **spot** from which the viewer looks at the painting; Western paintings seem to be more true to life, precision being obvious, while Chinese painter seeks close **resemblance** in spirit instead of accurate likeness in appearance.

12 Cooking

13 Western style of cooking is relatively more precise and scientific: how much water, salt, sugar and how many other **ingredients** are exactly needed for a certain dish. Besides, how many minutes and how strong the heat does the food need to be cooked are usually clearly stated. While to a great extent, roughness and experience are characteristics of Chinese cooking. A Chinese **recipe** will roughly tell you, a little oil, a little salt, etc. are needed , and you have no idea exactly how much each of the ingredients is. A Chinese usually senses how much by their experience and cooks delicious dishes. Look at the following description of how to prepare a piece of meat loaf in English.

1 Ib. ground beef

1 chopped onion

1 chopped green pepper

1 egg

1/2 cup tomato catsup

1 tablespoon mustard + 1 cup broken crackers

Place in a greased loaf pan and bake at 350°C for 1 hour.

14 **Concrete/Intuitive vs. Abstract/ Rational**

15 Thinking patterns in the East tend to be concrete or intuitive while thinking patterns in the West tend to be abstract or rational.

16 By quiet observation, self-experience, inspiration, insight without thorough logical thinking process, concrete or intuitive thinking patterns focus on thinking in images, sudden **enlightenment**.

17 Abstract thinking, also called logical or rational thought, is a mental process in which concept is used for judging and inferring.

18 Tortuous vs. Straight

19 Kalpan (1970) concluded that the problem-solving approaches and thinking patterns of English-speakers from the United States were more linear and direct than that of the Semitic, Asian, Romance language or Russian speakers. The Semitic individuals solved problems using a combination of **tangential** and semi-direct approaches. Asians employed a **circular** approach, Romans used a more consistently **circuitous** approach, and Russians employed a combination of direct and circuitous approaches (Fig 6.1).

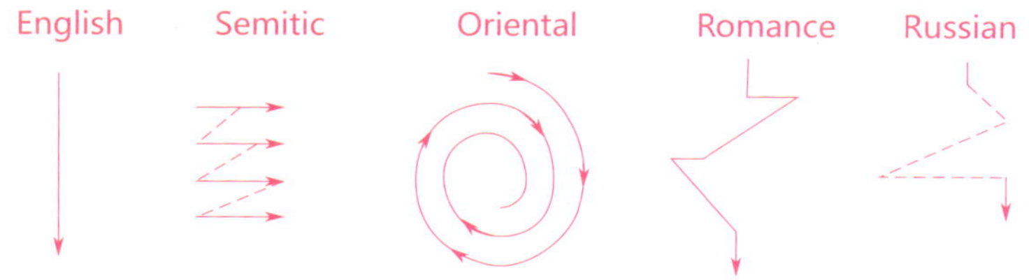

Fig 6.1 Thinking Patterns of Difference Cultures

20 In the Western philosophy, it has been a lasting convention to pursue alternate contrast in its reasoning, thus establishing a straightforward thinking pattern. But the Chinese, on the other hand, have been more accustomed to the harmony and unity of the world, especially that between the nature and the humans, and are more likely to adopt both sides of a matter, thus establishing a tortuous thinking pattern. As reflected in their speech, the English tend to stick to the point at the very beginning of the speech, offering a straight and frank theme of the speech before proceeding on to present the relevant details and accompanying situations. That may well account for the syntactic features of a compact head and a long and heavy ending with the emphasis at the front part of the sentences. And the Chinese sentences, due to the speakers' thinking modes, will present the relative information in great detail before hitting upon the theme, which **abound** in expressions with a long head with a short ending.

21 E.g. I met with my middle schoolmate at the entrance of the theater at 7: 30 yesterday evening , when I haven't seen for years. (昨天晚上 7 点半在剧院门口，我遇到了我多年未见的中学同学。)

22 In consequence of such thinking modes, the Chinese would organize their speech in logic order by telling the causes before describing the consequences, and offering some pre-positions before the deductive reasoning, and describing the facts before offering the speaker's attitude. And even in the spacious or sequential order, they tend to list from the more general to the more specific. As for the sequence of importance or significance, it's not difficult to see why they would begin with the most important or significant and then move on to the less important or less significant. The English speakers, with the assistance of conjunctions and prepositions, can be more flexible than the Chinese in this aspect.

synthetic	虚假的，不诚恳的	ingredient	成分，原料
intuitive	直观的，凭直觉的	recipe	食谱，烹饪法
concrete	具体的，实在的	enlightenment	启蒙，启迪
circumspect	谨慎的，周到的	tortuous	曲折的，复杂的
cosmos	宇宙	tangential	切线的，离题的
analytically	分析地，解析地	circular	圆形的，循环的
calligraphy	书法	circuitous	迂回的，曲折的
spot	地点，斑点	abound	大量存在，充满
resemblance	相似，相似之处		

Expanded Materials

Reading Comprehension

Which of the following thinking pattern mentioned in Text B is Chinese thinking pattern? Tick all you can find.

- [ ] Synthetic, intuitive, and concrete
- [ ] Analytical, statistical, and rational
- [ ] Whole
- [ ] Valuing subjectively
- [ ] Objective
- [ ] Specific and precise

Banked Cloze

Fill in the blanks by selecting suitable words from the word bank. You may not use any of the words more than once.

A. marital	B. expect	C. coexist
D. approach	E. specific	F. acquaintances

Americans use the word "friend" in a very general way. They may call both casual [1] ___________ and close companions "friends". Americans have school friends, work friends, sports friends and neighborhood friends. These friendships are based on common interests. When the shared activity ends, the friendship may fade. So, when making friends, it helps to have a good dose of cross-cultural understanding.

Here are just a few tips given by Americans to non-Americans who want to make friends with Americans:

1. Visit places Americans enjoy: parties, churches, Western restaurants, parks, sports clubs.

2. Be willing to take the first step. Don't wait for them to [2] ___________ you. Americans may not know if you speak English. They may be embarrassed if they can't speak your language.

3. Use small talk to open the conversation. Ask them where they're from, why they came to China, etc. Remember: Be careful to avoid personal questions about age, salary, [3] ___________ status and appearance.

4. Show an interest in their culture, their country or their job.(Americans like to talk about themselves!)

5. Invite them to join you for dinner or just for coffee or tea. Try to set a [4] ___________ time. Americans sometimes make general invitations like "Let's get together sometimes." Often this is just a way to be friendly. It is not always a real invitation.

6. Don't [5] ___________ too much at first. Maybe they're just being friendly. But maybe they do want to be your good friends. It will take time to tell.

Text C

Culture Shock

1 Culture shock is an experience a person may have when he or she moves to a culture which is different from his or her own; it is also personal disorientation a person may feel when experiencing an unfamiliar way of life due to immigration or a visit to a new country, a move between social environments, or simply transition to another type of life. One of the most common causes of culture shock involves individuals in a foreign environment. Culture shock can be described as consisting of at least one of the four distinct phases: honeymoon, negotiation, adjustment, and adaptation.

2 Common problems include: information overload, language barrier, generation gap, technology gap, skill interdependence, formulation dependency, homesickness (cultural), infinite regress (homesickness), boredom (job dependency), response ability (cultural skill set). There is no true way to entirely prevent culture shock, as individuals in any society are personally affected by cultural

contrasts differently.

3 **Five Phases of Culture Shock**

4 Anthropologist Kalvero Oberg listed five stages of the W-curve for culture shock (Fig 6.2).

5 1. Honeymoon (Euphoria/Excitement)

6 During this period, the differences between the old and new culture are seen in a romantic light. For example, in moving to a new country, an individual might love the new food, the pace of life, and the locals' habits. During the first few weeks, most people are fascinated by the new culture. They associate with nationals who speak their language, and who are polite to the foreigners. Like most honeymoon periods, this stage eventually ends.

7 2. Crisis

8 After some time (usually around three months, depending on the individual), differences between the old and new culture become apparent and may create anxiety. Excitement may eventually give way to unpleasant feelings of frustration and anger as one continues to experience unfavorable events that may be perceived as strange and offensive to one's cultural attitude. Language barriers, stark differences in public hygiene, traffic safety, food accessibility and quality may heighten the sense of disconnection from the surroundings.

9 While being transferred into a different environment puts special pressure on communication skills, there are practical difficulties to overcome, such as circadian rhythm disruption that often leads to **insomnia** and daylight drowsiness; adaptation of **gut flora** to different bacteria levels and concentrations in food and water; difficulty in seeking treatment for illness, as medicines may have different names from the native country's and the same active ingredients might be hard to recognize.

10 Still, the most important change in the period is communication: People adjusting to a new culture often feel lonely and homesick because they are not yet used to the new environment and meeting people with whom they are not familiar every day. The language barrier may become a major obstacle in creating new relationships: Special attention must be paid to one's and others' culture-specific body language signs, linguistic **faux pas**, conversation tone, linguistic nuances and customs, and false friends.

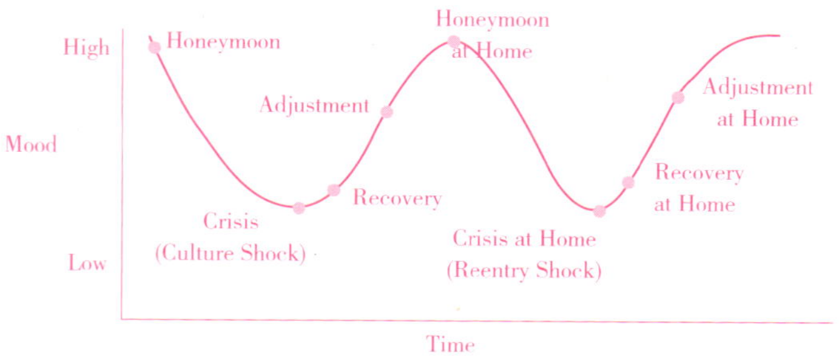

Fig 6.2 "W-curve" for Culture Shock
Based on Oberg (1960) and Gallahom & Gallahorn (1963)

11 In the case of students studying abroad, some develop additional symptoms of loneliness that ultimately affect their lifestyles as a whole. Due to the strain of living in a different country without parental support, international students often feel anxious and feel more pressure while adjusting to new cultures — even more so when the cultural distances are wide, as patterns of logic and speech are different and a special emphasis is put on rhetoric.

12 3. Reintegration (Recovery)

13 Some may go through the stage of **deculturation** while others the **acculturation**. Deculturation refers to the process of taking away people's original traits. Acculturation is the process of social, psychological, and cultural change that stems from **blending** between cultures.

14 4. Adjustment (Autonomy)

15 Again, after some time (usually 6 to 12 months), one grows accustomed to the new culture and develops routines. One knows what to expect in most situations and the host country no longer feels all that new. One becomes concerned with basic living again, and things become more "normal". One starts to develop problem-solving skills for dealing with the culture and begins to accept the culture's ways with a positive attitude. The culture begins to make sense, and negative reactions and responses to the culture arc reduced.

16 5. Independence

17 In the mastery stage individuals are able to participate fully and comfortably in the host culture. Mastery does not mean total conversion; people often keep many traits from their earlier culture, such as accents and languages. It is often referred to as the **bicultural** stage.

18 But not everyone goes through all the stages mentioned above and not everyone experiences extreme culture shocks.

19 **Reverse Culture Shock**

20 Reverse culture shock (also known as "re-entry shock" or "own culture shock") may take place — returning to one's home culture after growing accustomed to a new one can produce the same effects as described above. These are results from the psychosomatic and psychological consequences of the readjustment process to the primary culture. The affected person often finds this more surprising and difficult to deal with than the original culture shock. This phenomenon, the reactions that members of the re-entered culture exhibit towards the re-entrant, and the inevitability of the two are encapsulated in the following saying, which is also the title of a book by Thomas Wolfe, *You Can't Go Home Again*.

21 Reverse culture shock is generally made up of two parts: idealization and expectation. When an extended period of time is spent abroad we focus on the good from our past, cutout the bad, and create an idealized version of the past. Secondly, once removed from our familiar setting and placed in a foreign one we incorrectly assume that our previous world has not changed. We expect things to remain exactly the same as when we left them. The realization that life back home is now

different, that the world has continued without us, and the process of readjusting to these new conditions as well as actualizing our new perceptions about the world with our old way of living causes discomfort and psychological anguish.

22 **Think and Discuss**

23 As an invaluable asset to the world, Chinese culture is diverse and unique. Throughout its history, it has exerted global influence on philosophy, morals, etiquette, language, ceramics, architecture, music, dance, literature, martial arts, cuisine, the arts and politics. Share with your partner the aspects of Chinese culture that you most admire. Prepare a 3-minute speech on Chinese culture and its influence on the world and present it to the class. Remember to organize your speech chronologically.

24 ★What do you think are the essences of traditional Chinese culture?

25 ★Give two examples to illustrate how traditional Chinese values have influenced China's development today.

26 **Cultural Kaleidoscope**

27 **At home with food**

28 Sometimes, the best way to feel at home is with food! When we're in another country, we can miss our home comforts. When I first visited China, I tried lots of dishes like hotpot in Beijing. It's so different from English cuisine and also different from the Chinese food I had in the UK. The food doesn't have such strong **flavors** as it does in its home country. I was not used to these flavors, so I started to feel culture shock. Then I went on to Shanghai. At a small street stall, I saw the gold-bottomed Shengjianbao (Fig 6.3) sitting in a pot. I had to try it! When I bit into one, the juice **poured out**. So many flavors filled my mouth. These flavors were new, but there was also something familiar about them.

29 Shengjianbao is like a British pork pie (Fig 6.4). They both have **minced** meat and **seasonings** as well as a long history. But the pan-fried bun is cooked in **dough** while the British pork pie is put in **pastry**. Now, whenever I visit Shanghai, Shengjianbao must be on the menu. I know they'll always make me feel right at home.

Fig 6.3　Shanghai Shengjianbao

Fig 6.4　British Pork Pie

insomnia	失眠	flavors	味道
gut flora	肠道菌群	pour out	涌出
faux pas	失礼，过失	minced	切碎的
deculturation	文化剥离，文化丧失	seasonings	调味品
acculturation	文化适应，文化同化	dough	面团
blending	混合，融合	pastry	油酥面团
bicultural	双文化的，两种文化并存的		

Expanded Materials

Expanded Materials

Reading Comprehension

Each of the following statements contions information in Text C. Decide whether the statement is true(T) or false(F) based on the text.

1. People adjusting to a new culture often feel lonely and homesick because they are not used to the new environment and meeting people with whom they are not familiar every day.
2. Deculturation is the process of social, psychological, and cultural change that stems from blending between cultures.
3. Reverse culture shock is generally made up of two parts: adaptation and expectations.

Discussion

1. How will you imagine what you would experience if you were studying abroad?
2. How does culture shock affect people who are exposed to a new cultural environment?

Text D

Chinese Students in the United States

1 It seems to me that majority of Chinese students in the United States have never made the effort to reach out and embrace American life on its own terms. Instead, most share apartments with one or more fellow Chinese students, speaking Chinese and eating Chinese food on a daily basis. In some respects, it is as if these students had never left China. **Interactions** with Americans tend to be limited to relatively formal, academic settings, such as the classroom or a professor's office.

2 Moreover, few Chinese students participate in campus-wide **extracurricular** activities, such as athletic matches and dances, which would put them into contact with a diverse array of American young people. Rather, most limit themselves to taking part in programs arranged by the Chinese Students Association and, naturally, these events are generally linked to uniquely Chinese occasions such as the Spring Festival and National Day. As a result, even Chinese students who have spent years in the United States often find it difficult to engage American friends in **sophisticated** conversations about such subjects as American politics, popular music, etc. In short, they lack a "feel" for the country.

3 Fundamentally, few Chinese see the chance to study in a foreign country for what it is a once-in-a-lifetime-opportunity to get to know another country from the inside. Chinese students typically focus so **single-mindedly** on their studies that they lose sight of the larger picture, that is, their ultimate role as cultural interpreters between their homeland and the foreign country. To be sure, a Chinese student's service as an engineer or a biologist is integral to China's continued economic construction; but his or her ability to bridge the divide — or often, the perceived divide between two distinct cultures is perhaps even more important over the long run.

4 I believe that the next generation of Chinese students in the United States will recognize their crucial function in the process of furthering US-China understanding. They will return to China in greater numbers to contribute to their country's development in many more ways. I only hope that before these students find their way back to China, they find their way into the heart of America.

interaction	交流	sophisticated	复杂的，水平高的
extracurricular	课外的，课程以外的	single-mindedly	一心一意地，专心致志地

Discussion

1. What do you think of the American's description of Chinese students in the USA? Why do many Chinese students behave in the way described above?
2. What should Chinese students do to prepare for the life in another country? And what should we do to help enhance understanding between different peoples?

Expanded Materials

Suggestions for Further Reading

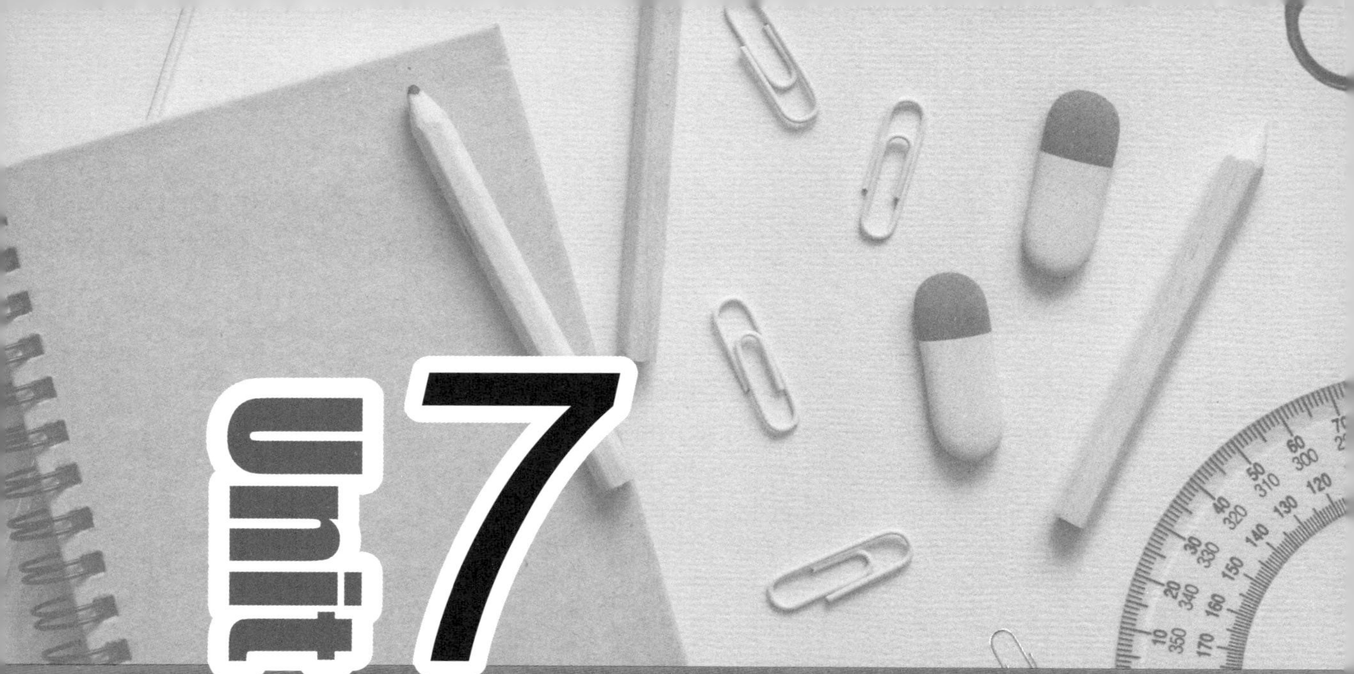

Unit 7

Cultural Differences in Education

Where three men walk together, I can learn from one.

— ***Confucius***

Learning Objectives

At the end of this unit, you should be able to:

- analyze cultural influence on the education context;
- critically identify the educational differences in different countries and know how to deal with these differences.

Warm-up Activities

1 Case Study I

Karen had been teaching high school English in the United States before she accepted a teaching job at a teacher's college in China. She found her new environment and her new teaching assignment exciting. Both her students and her colleagues seemed a bit shy of her, but Karen was sure that in time they would all come to be friends.

In the classroom, however, Karen was very frustrated. When she asked a question, the class was silent. Only if she called on a particular student would she get an answer, often a very good one. She could not understand why they wouldn't volunteer when they obviously knew the answers. They were very quiet when she was speaking in front of the class, and never asked questions, let alone interrupt with an opinion, but as soon as the class ended, they would cluster around her desk to ask their questions one-by-one. They would also offer their suggestions about the lesson at this time.

Karen often asked her students to work in small groups during class, especially when they were editing each other's writing. They were slow to move into groups and when they did, they often simply formed a group with the people sitting next to them. Most frustrating of all, after she taught her class how to edit essays, she found that the students were likely to write vague and not very helpful remarks on their classmates' papers. They would say nice things about the essays and correct small grammatical errors, but seemed unwilling to criticize them in a way that would help another student revise the essay.

Questions:

1. Do you often behave in the same way in class as the students in the case above? Why?
2. What kind of cultural phenomenon can be reflected in the case above?

2 Case Study II

Tom is an overseas student from the US who is now learning Chinese in a university in south China. After learning a few daily expressions and the pronunciation of Chinese in Pinyin, it's time for him to learn how to write the Chinese characters.

In the class, Ms. Zhang, his Chinese teacher asked him to write down some Chinese characters on the blackboard by imitation. After trying a few times, Tom still couldn't do it well. Spotting this, Ms. Zhang said to him, "You should follow the sequences of the strokes and do it exactly like this." To Ms. Zhang's anger, Tom seemed unhappy and answered, "Why should I? I don't want to. I want to do it in my own way."

Questions:

1. Why did Ms. Zhang feel angry?
2. Why did Tom feel unhappy? Did he mean to offend Ms. Zhang?

Text A

Educational Differences in Various Cultures

1 Most cultures that have formal educational systems teach much the same content-reading, mathematics, writing, and so forth — but educational differences can be found in what a culture emphasizes and how the content is taught. Each culture, whether consciously or unconsciously, tends to glorify its historical, scientific, and artistic accomplishments and to minimize the accomplishments of other culture. In this way, schools in all cultures, whether they intend to or not, teach ethnocentrism.

2 As we examine the specific aspects of what and how cultures teach, it will, of course, be impossible to include every cultural educational system. Fortunately, we need not cover them all in order to make our point: culture influences education. To this end, we explore the educational systems of Republic of Korea, Japan, the United States, Mexico and to see what and how cultures are taught.

3 **Education in Republic of Korea**

4 In Republic of Korea, all schools follow the same program of study. The curriculum content is determined by the Ministry of Education. There are few electives in middle schools and high schools, and variations are tailored to the type of school a student attends. Schools take a variety of forms. There are general schools, vocational schools, or specialized school, and assignment is based on regional examination and lottery. Children learn both Korean and Chinese characters in elementary school. English, as well as an additional foreign language, is required in middle school and high school.

5 In addition to standard subjects, the schools emphasize moral education. Teachers are expected to assume leadership in these areas, and parents hold teachers are responsible for disciplining their children. The students engage in several typical classroom behaviors. They typically "show respect by avoiding eye contact, bowing, and not initiating conversation with an elder".

6 **Education in Japan**

7 The Sino-Japanese and Russo-Japanese wars between 1894 and 1905 increased Japanese nationalistic feelings. Japan also

experienced accelerated modernization and industrialization. In accord with the government's new nationalism and efforts to modernize the country, educational reform was sought. The Japanese education system took as its model the Western European educational systems, especially that of Germany. But the basic ideology of education remained the traditional one outlined in 1890 in the Imperial Rescript on Education. In 1900 the period of ordinary elementary schooling was set at four years, and schooling was made compulsory for all children.

8 Education in Japan is relatively homogeneous and set by national standardized curriculum that "emphasizes social studies, democratic political processes, and religious tolerance". Reading, writing, and mathematics are emphasized, while oral language is not. This lack of practice in oral skills often causes Japanese students to experience serious problems when they attend school in the United States.

9 Education is a high national priority because the Japanese believe that "the best way to ensure their future is to develop their most valued natural resource — their people". Because of this value placed on education, the Japanese have a correspondingly high regard for educators. Teachers have a reciprocal responsibility to the community.

10 Education in the United States

11 It is an accepted truism that the world is facing a major population explosion. The schools in the United States have been greatly affected by the combination of population and immigration increase. Schools in the United States have attempted to respond to the diversity now found in most classrooms.

12 The gap between whites' and minorities' test scores has narrowed, which may well be attributed to educators who daily confront diversity in their classrooms and have identified the central issues in the education of a culturally diverse population, such as learning style difference, language diversity and gender. Besides that, multi-cultural teaching competences and technology also play important roles in the education of the US.

13 Education in Mexico

14 Education in Mexico is very different from the educational systems in Republic of Korea, Japan, and the United States. Mexico's educational system mandates the students complete the twelfth grade; however, because of the harsh economic climate in that country, students often can't do this. As is the case with most educational system, history is emphasized. The arts, trade, vocational skills, and Mexican cultural values are stringently emphasized.

15 There are fewer teachers in the Mexican school system, and classes are very large. In Mexican society, the teacher has significant status and holds a prominent place in the ordered hierarchy. As well as being academic instructors, Mexican teachers are friends with their students.

16 Several behaviors and dynamics dominate the Mexican classroom. First, because Mexican children grow up within cooperative environments that emphasize strong family ties, the school continues to reinforce this primary

value. Second, the Mexican culture values conversation, so the students enthusiastically participate in classroom discussions. Finally, Mexicans value the present. Mexican students are more concerned with doing a job well, regardless of the amount of time required.

Reading Comprehension

Each of the following statements contains information in Text A. Decide whether the statement is true (T) or false (F) based on the text.

1. Every culture is inclined to glorify its historical, scientific, and artistic accomplishments and to minimize the accomplishments of other culture.
2. Children learn both Korean and English in elementary school in Republic of Korea.
3. The students show respect by avoiding eye contact, bowing, and not initiating conversation with an elder in Republic of Korea.
4. Japanese students have no problems when they attend school in the United States because the US teachers have multi-cultural teaching competences.
5. Mexican children grow up within cooperative environments that emphasize strong family ties, and the school continues to reinforce this primary value.

Text B

Would Chinese-style Education Work on British Kids?

1 In 2015, a BBC television documentary *Are Our Kids Tough Enough: Chinese School* was released. As across-border collaboration, it was both an educational experiment and a creative exercise. The BBC invited five Chinese teachers to Bohunt School, a successful secondary school located in Hampshire UK, to teach a group of 50 9th grade students one month the worth of "Chinese education lessons", from morning exercises, the flag-raising ceremony and wearing oversized school uniform to eye exercises, afternoon extra meals and evening study, all according to the schedule of Chinese students. In the month-long crossover, a series of conflicts between the Chinese and British cultures, educational systems, educational philosophy, and the social climate become the main theme throughout the film.

2 This documentary has raised the attention and stimulated the interest of both Chinese and British media, education scholars and policy makers. Neil Strowger, head of the Bohunt School, told the *Times*, the Chinese teachers are "providing content for students to memorise

and they **regurgitate** it in an exam", which is "not to work with them in any way".

3 "No real questioning or no opportunities for the students to work in pairs or in groups," he is also quoted by the *Times* as saying, "it was entirely **didactic**, delivered from the front of teachers, hour after hour."

4 It's true that in China, both students and teachers attach so much importance to grades and qualifications that they don't want to "waste" time on practical training. They spend countless time doing test papers, with the faith that "grades mean everything". The significance of exams dates back to the day when the Imperial Examination started in year 605 as the civil service examination system provided equal opportunities for all candidates to be selected into the government and thereafter to change their destinies. Chinese students are fully aware of the competitiveness in the society the moment after they get into primary schools. The significance of ranking and grade remained the same to Gaokao, i.e. the National Higher Education Entrance Examination.

5 Despite the dramatic show of the conflicts between Chinese teachers and British students, many British Twitter users complained about their own education system rather than that used by the Chinese teachers. "They are right. British education has gone soft. Teachers are abused and students have no discipline... The public see it but the politicians don't." Meanwhile, a number of Chinese netizens, especially those of the Post-70s and Post-80s generation, considered that the teaching method that neglected the student's personality in the documentary was familiar to them. Student autonomy, questioning and the development of skills to allow students to think for themselves, key elements in British pedagogical approaches, do not appear to be part of the Chinese approach.

6 In the age of globalization, it is trendy that education could become globalized as well. It is always helpful for school leaders to learn from different systems, and the best teachers are continually questioning how best to teach their students. It would be more effective to learn from each other and adapt it to one's own education system. For instance, Chinese education system needs to pay more attention to students' practical experiences, independent research skill and critical evaluation ability, focusing on the cultivation of students' self-confidence, cooperation, independent learning and creativity. On the other hand, British education system could consider raising students' level in math or science by guiding them to develop certain learning skills and reinforce their abilities through more practices.

regurgitate 反刍，照搬　　didactic 说教的，教导的

Reading Comprehension

Fill in the chart based on your own understanding of China's education.

Behavior in Class	Agree/Disagree	Cultural Values
Passive in leaning		
Not encouraged to ask questions		
Not encouraged to respond		
Expect to get the answer from teachers		
Learn for examination		
Teachers are authoritarian		
No personal opinion or perspective		
No participation in seminars		

Discussion

1. Have you watched the BBC television documentary *Are Our Kids Tough Enough: Chinese School*? Do you think the documentary reflect the real conflicts between British and Chinese educational methods?
2. Do you think education will be globalized? Why or why not?

Text C

Introduction of Western Learning to Modern China

1 In the Chinese history, Western learning was introduced to China for three times. The first group of Christians who came to China in the late Ming Dynasty were called the Jesuits and they were Catholics. Knowing that the Chinese thought highly of their own culture while disregarding other cultures, Matteo Ricci, the representative of the Jesuits, tried hard to adapt to Chinese culture by wearing the Confucian robe, learning Chinese language, and showing respect for Confucianism. The approach he used was named accommodation strategy. Since the Chinese showed little interest in Christianity, yet were much interested in the products of modern science, Ricci took advantage of teaching them the scientific knowledge about **cartography**, mechanic clocks, etc. while spreading Christianity. The so-called scholarly mission was quite effective and the missionaries gained respect and trust

from both Chinese emperor and officials. For instance, the world map brought by Ricci dispelled the Chinese old view on the world, that was, "The sky is round and the earth is square" or China as the center of the world. The new notions like earth, five continents, the Pacific Ocean , the Atlantic Ocean, and the Mediterranean Seas shown in the **Kunyu Wanguo Quantu** drawn by Matteo Ricci clearly indicated that China was only a part of the world, but not the center of the world. Since the previous cosmology the Chinese held was the foundation of Chinese centralism, people's perception of the Hua-Yi distinction began to falter. The Jesuits after Matteo Ricci also helped the Chinese change to a new calendar and build a modern observatory.

2 However, during the reign of Emperor Kangxi, the Vatican changed their mind and stopped the Jesuits from accommodating Chinese culture. All the converts were not allowed to worship Confucius any longer because God was the only one they should **venerate**. The so-called **Rites Dispute** led Kangxi to ban the Jesuits from coming to China and the following emperor Yongzheng completely banned the Christians from coming to China. The interruption lasted more than one hundred and thirty years and it wasn't until the early 19th century when Robert Morrison came to China that renewed the Christian missions to China. But this time, they were mostly Protestant missionaries. Robert Morrison was the first Protestant who came to China in 1807.

3 Robert Morrison was trained to be a foreign missionary and his target country was China. The school where he received training provided both general education and special missionary education because its head, David Bogue, was a liberal-minded person and he fully understood that the more extensive one's knowledge range was, the easier for the missionary to survive in an unexpected condition because he could find a job using his knowledge so as to carry on his mission. This humanistic teaching approach had much to do with the slogan of the Enlightenment, i.e. "Knowledge is power" and a practical mind advocated by Thomas Reid in his theory of realism.

4 Upon his arrival in China in 1807, Morrison meticulously followed the instructions given by David Bogue at Gosport Academy. The first thing Morrison did was to find a native Chinese to teach him the language. Morrison endured years of solitude and hardships but with his fortitude he established the Anglo-Chinese College in Malacca in 1818, which was moved to Hong Kong in 1843. Now with the name of **Ying Wa College**, the college is the oldest school in Hong Kong with over 200 years of history. The curriculum designed for Anglo-Chinese College followed the Gosport example and taught "reading, writing, singing...arithmetic, geography, history of the world, etc." Morrison did not live to see full functioning of the school because he died in 1834. But his pedagogical idea was passed down to the following schools built by the Morrison Fund to support education in China.

5 Morrison School helped in its own way in the termination of Chinese old-style private education, the adaptation of the modern

education system in terms of division of classes, course objectives, course content, approaches, and the abolishment of the Imperial Civil Service Examination.

6 The original purpose of Protestant missionaries who came to China was to propagate Christianity and everything they did was pointing at the same goal. But the byproduct of those activities was a complete introduction of the Western education system, printing press, and the way of thinking to the Chinese people so that China's modernization was promoted through this kind of cultural exchanges. After the death of Robert Morrison, Morrison School became a model for general education and began to flourish in China.

7 In 1895, Sheng Xuanhuai submitted his memorial to Emperor Guangxu to request for approval to set up a modern higher education institution in Tianjin. After approval on October 2, 1895, Peiyang Western Study College was founded by him and American educator Charles Daniel Tenney and later developed to Peiyang University. It was the first university providing four-year degree modern higher education in China. The university modeled itself on the famous American universities and aimed to rejuvenate China by training qualified personnel with new scientific and technological knowledge. Charles Daniel Tenney, a missionary from the USA, was the first President of Peiyang University in Tianjin, China from 1895 through 1906.

8 Following the introduction of general education to the 19th century Qing Dynasty, professional education, i.e. medical education also entered China, but it was accompanied by the medical missionary introduced by American Protestants, with whose help, several modern hospitals were successfully established in big cities such as Beijing and Guangzhou. Even today, both Beijing Union Medical College and Beijing Union Hospital are ranked at the top of medical schools and hospitals in China.

cartography	制图学，绘图法	Rites Dispute	礼仪之争
Kunyu Wanguo Quantu	坤舆万国全图	Ying Wa College	英华书院
venerate	崇敬，敬重，敬仰		

Banked Cloze

Fill in the blanks by selecting suitable words from the word bank. You may not use any of the words more than once.

A. privilege	B. established	C. generous	D. favor	E. biased
F. traced	G. justice	H. feudal	I. acknowledged	J. fatal

Many Chinese scholars believe the history of education in China can be [1] __________ back at as far as the 16th century BC. Throughout this period of time, education was the [2] __________ of the elites. The teachings of Confucianism during the Spring and Autumn and Warring States periods, were mainly based on "The Four Books" and "The Five Classics". "The Four Books" and "The Five Classics" were the [3] __________ subjects of the Confucian culture in the [4] __________ society in ancient China. "The Four Books" refers to *The Great Learning*, *The Doctrine of the Mean*, *Confucian Analects* and *The Works of Mencius*. And "The Five Classics" includes *The Book of Poetry* (also known as *The Book of Songs*, *The Book of Odes*), *The Book of History*, *The Book of Rites*, *The Book of Changes*, and *The Spring and Autumn Annals*.

Confucianism probably is the biggest influence in education of China throughout the entire Chinese history. Later in Han Dynasty, a form of public education system was [5] __________. Not only elites from upper class families can study in school, a common man can also use education as a path to become a better man, known as a gentleman.

In Confucianism, a gentleman considers what is right, when the peasant considers what will pay. A gentleman trusts in [6] __________ and the peasant trusts in favor. A gentleman is [7] __________ and fair, when the peasant is [8] __________ and petty. A gentleman looks within for guidance and the peasant looks unto others. A gentleman is easy to serve, and hard to please. The peasant is hard to serve, and easy to please. A gentleman is to know what we know, and know what we do not know.

Discussion

Text C is mainly about the introduction of Western education to modern China. Do you think Chinese culture has influenced Western education all the same? Do you have any example to support your viewpoint?

Text D

Confucius Institute and the HSK

1 Seeking to promote study of Chinese culture and language and to forge positive bonds with educators and students, China's government began sponsoring the establishment of Confucius Institutes overseas since 2004.

2 The Confucius Institute (CI) aims to promote the spread of the Chinese language, deepen people's understanding of the Chinese

language and culture worldwide, push forward educational cooperation and cultural exchange between China and the rest of the world, and enhance understanding between different groups of people across the world. It is a non-profit education program jointly founded by all of its partners in compliance with the principles of mutual respect, friendly consultation, equality, and mutual benefit.

3 The Confucius Institute is named after the noted Chinese philosopher Confucius (551 BC–479 BC). Confucius has been portrayed as a teacher, advisor, editor, philosopher, reformer, and prophet. The name Confucius, a Latinized combination of the surname Kong "孔" with an honorific suffix "Master" (fuzi, 夫子), and his casting as a **progenitor** of "Eastern" thought in Early Modern Europe, make him arguably the most significant thinker in East Asian history.

4 "Confucius Institute" is a trademarked brand name. By borrowing the name Confucius, it created a brand that was instantly recognized as a symbol of Chinese culture. Many countries have established language and culture promotion organizations such as **Portugal's Instituto Camões, Britain's British Council, France's Alliance Française, Italy's Società Dante Alighieri, Spain's Instituto Cervantes and Germany's Goethe-Institut** — several of them named for an iconic cultural figure identified with that country, as Confucius is identified with China.

5 The first Confucius Institute opened on 21 November 2004 in Seoul, Republic of Korea, after establishing a pilot institute in Tashkent, Uzbekistan in June 2004. The second Confucius Institute was opened on the campus of the University of Maryland, College Park, also in November 2004. As of 2019, there were 530 Confucius Institutes in dozens of countries on six continents.

6 However, Hanban, a non-profit government organization connected with the Ministry of Education, which used to be responsible for the headquarters of CI, was considered to have close ties to a number of senior CPC officials by many foreigners. With the boost of China's economy, some suspicious people who begin to regard China as a threat doubted about the intention of the Chinese government to set up CI. Some CIs are becoming inactive and some are closed.

7 In July 2020, Hanban announced its re-naming to Center for Language Education and Cooperation, stating that the Confucius Institute was fully handed over to Chinese International Education Foundation. Founded in Beijing in June 2020, Chinese International Education Foundation is a non-profit charitable social organization registered at the Ministry of Civil Affairs of the People's Republic of China. Jointly initiated by 27 universities, enterprises, and social organizations, the Foundation is dedicated to supporting projects of Chinese International Education worldwide, promoting people-to-people exchanges, enhancing understanding among countries, and thus contributing to mutual learning and exchanges between the diverse civilizations in the world and to building a community of shared future for mankind.

8 Foreigners from different countries across continents choose to take Chinese classes

in CI have different goals: to get to know more friends, to have a glimpse of Chinese culture, to help pass the HSK to later find job opportunities in China...The name HSK is an acronym for the name of the exam in Chinese, which is "汉语水平考试" (Hànyǔ Shuǐpíng Kǎoshì). The HSK is an international standardized test for Chinese proficiency established to assess the Chinese proficiency of non-native Chinese speakers (including foreigners, overseas Chinese, ethnic Chinese and Chinese minority candidates). This exam is used to measure how well test-takers can use the Chinese language in their daily, academic and professional lives. The test is most commonly used in China and is only available in simplified Chinese.

9 The original version of the exam consisted of 11 levels, which makes it difficult to promote outside of China. The high number of levels also made it hard to determine how the HSK corresponded to the language testing standards of other countries. Therefore, in 2009, the exam underwent major changes, paving the way for the New HSK. This test was released in 2010 and consists of the 6 levels. HSK 6 is the highest level and candidates who pass this level should be able to easily understand what they hear or read in Chinese, and express their opinions fluently in Chinese in oral or written form.

10 The HSK is a prerequisite for studying at any Chinese University, unless the course is taught 100% in English. Depending on the university and the degree in question, candidates usually need to have an HSK 4 certificate as the minimum language requirement for studying for an undergraduate degree, and a level 5 certification for postgraduate studies. More prestigious universities such as Peking University may even require level 6. A higher level can also enhance the chance for the test-taker to obtain any type of Chinese government scholarship.

11 From the introduction of Western learning to the promotion of Chinese culture abroad, China has shown the determination to join the colorful garden of world civilization actively. Cultural differences will not disappear, but more and more bridges can be constructed in the long run, to connect the gaps between the differences. Education provides the building blocks for the construction of these bridges.

progenitor 祖先，先驱

Portugal's Instituto Camões, Britain's British Council, France's Alliance Française, Italy's Società Dante Alighieri, Spain's Instituto Cervantes and Germany's Goethe-Institut: 葡萄牙卡蒙斯学院、英国文化教育协会、法语联盟、意大利但丁语言学院、西班牙塞万提斯学院和德国歌德学院

Reading Comprehension

Each of the following statements contains information in Text D. Decide whether the statement is true (T) or false (F) based on the text.

___ 1. Cervantes is an iconic cultural figure in Spain, just as Camões in Italy.

___ 2. The first Confucius Institute opened on 21 November 2004 in Tashkent, Uzbekistan.

___ 3. Chinese International Education Foundation has been responsible for the headquarters of the Confucius Institute since 2020.

___ 4. The HSK is an international standardized test for Chinese proficiency established to assess the Chinese proficiency of non-native Chinese speakers.

___ 5. HSK 6 was the highest level in 2008 and candidates who pass this level should be able to easily understand Chinese when they went to Beijing to Olympic Games.

Discussion

What is the significance of establishing Confucius Institutes abroad?

Suggestions for Further Reading

Unit 8

Culture and International Business

Despite popular beliefs to the contrary, the single greatest barrier to business success is the one erected by culture.

— E. T. Hall & M. R. Hall

Learning Objectives

At the end of this unit, you should be able to:

- learn useful business-related words and expressions;
- understand the influence of culture in negotiation and management;
- recognize varied negotiation styles from culture to culture;
- develop skills in intercultural communication in business context.

Warm-up Activities

1 Case Study I

In 1992, a business delegation from China arrived in the United States to purchase a technical equipment worth US$ 3 million. Before signing the purchase contract, the United States business negotiators tried to please the business delegates from China by presenting each a beautifully decorated box with a carefully-selected gift inside. However, when each business representative from China opened the box in accordance with U.S. custom, everyone's smiling face froze. It turned out that inside the elaborate box is a golf cap, and the color is green. The US negotiators were confused with the sudden loss of friendly facial expression and the talk broke down in the end.

Questions:

1. Why did the business delegates from China stop smiling when they see the gifts from the US negotiators?
2. What different meanings do you know conveyed by "green cap" in various cultures?

2 Case Study II

A U.S. manufacturing firm bought a textile machine factory in Birmingham, England. In an attempt to make the workers in their new factory more productive, the U.S. managers wanted to shorten the time consuming tea break to which all workers were entitled. In England, a tea break can take a half-hour per man, as each worker brews his own tea to his particular taste and sips out of a large, pint size vessel with the indulgence of a wine taster. The managers tried to speed up the "sipping time" to ten minutes. They went ahead and installed a tea-vending machine — just put a paper cup under the spigot and out pours a standard brew. The pint sized container was replaced by a five-ounce cup printed — as they are in America — with morale-building messages imploring greater dedication to the job and loyalty to the company. Then one Monday morning the workers rioted. Windows were broken, epithets greeted the managers as they entered the factory and police had to be called to restore order. The factory never did get back into production. Even after the tea-brewing machine was hauled out, workers boycotted the company and it finally closed down.

Questions:

1. What made the workers riot and boycott the US company?
2. What do you think the US managers should have done to make the workers more productive?

Text A

Cross-cultural Negotiation

1 As businesses operate in an increasingly globalized world, international business people find themselves working in multicultural environment, in which culture plays an unneglectable role and sometimes even makes a difference. The "green cap" story shows us a failed negotiation caused by the lack of cultural sensitivity.

2 Negotiation is the communication that takes place in order to reach agreement about how to handle both common and conflicting interests between two or more parties. Even in your own country, to negotiate productively is extremely difficult dealing with colleagues who think like you, process information as you do, share a common set of values and speak the same language. Now consider a situation where there is little shared knowledge, few common values and a different language is spoken, and you can readily see just how complicated negotiating international transactions can become.

3 Some people may assume that negotiating skills are value free and are the same around the world, like the rules of chess. Not only does this view mistakenly discount the role of culture in framing the priorities of negotiators, it also overlooks what happens when people of different cultures interact. The interaction produces a communication situation that is the product of both cultures and of the personalities of both teams. Negotiation, like all communication, is dynamic and not static. People from different cultures have different communication styles, different strategies for persuasion and a different set of **protocols**. Differences occur in the way a conflict is viewed, managed, and resolved. The art of international negotiation **boils down to** this simple concept: the interaction of two sides pursuing one goal — profit — through divergent methods. To negotiate effectively, you not only need special communication skills; you also need to understand your own culture and the other party's culture. You need to be able to switch from behavior you are used to within your own culture to the behavior that will be most appropriate for another culture.

4 You should develop a negotiating plan that will minimize the potential of misunderstanding and conflict. You need to take cultural sensitivities into consideration in order to en-

hance the chances of reaching an agreement — and forming a business relationship — that will endure beyond the initial contract.

5 All interactions with other cultures become more likely to succeed when you know something about the other culture's strategy differences and expectations. You can identify these cultural factors by posing some questions about an unfamiliar culture: what is the best way to organize and structure the negotiation communication and how best to persuade; taking into account the nonverbal and behavioral signals involved, the way decisions are made, information is collected, and problems are solved in the other culture. In many ways, the negotiation communication task is a **cumulative** one.

6 There are two basic approaches to how a final outcome is viewed. Some cultures view the negotiating process as a "win-win" situation (Fig 8.1) — a process through which both sides gain. Other cultures adopt a zero sum mentality, where someone's gain must always equal someone's loss. The sum of the net gain and net loss is always zero. Individuals from cultures that view negotiation through this "win-lose" **prism** see the process as a series of confrontational battles to be either won or lost. Individuals from the "win-win" perspective instead view negotiations as a collaborative effort seeking to maximize total gain. Confrontation, as this side sees it, is counter productive. Trying to convince win-lose practitioners that a win-win strategy is possible is usually difficult. Sellers often prefer to project a win-win approach while buyers tend towards the zero sum game (Fig 8.2).

Fig 8.1 Win-win Negotiation

Fig 8.2 Zero Sum Game

7 When locked in negotiations it is important to take into consideration the differences in the decision-making process between cultures. In some cultures with individualistic values (United States, Australia) decisions can be made quickly — and often by a single individual. However, in cultures with collectivist values (Japan, China), decisions are made by consensus and can take longer. However, implementation of decisions is quicker in collectivist cultures, as opposed to individualistic cultures that often demand the right to question the decision handed down.

8 The most critical phase for an international venture is the first negotiation, and thus extensive preparation is critical. A learn-as-you-go approach can be deadly. For instance, it is essential to understand the importance of rank in the other country; to know who the decision makers are; to be familiar with the

business style of the foreign company; and to know the issues well. And you have to develop a profile of your negotiating opponents: are they task-driven or relationship-driven? How do they process information? Are they from a high-context or low-context culture? What are the important issues in their culture? Is their communication style direct or indirect?

9 Differences in language use also have to be taken into consideration. In the process of intercultural negotiation, you should always look for problems in the written documents stemming from any meeting or agreement. Translation can be imprecise and the whole sense or structure of a deal can be altered by the use or substitution of a single word in a written document. Documents and contracts should be provided in both languages (even if you use a common language to negotiate). It is essential, though, that you have a member of your staff or a professional translator who is fluent in the other language compare the translations to ensure no ambiguity.

10 In order for negotiations to be successful, the negotiations must allow for both parties to gain something — a win-win situation — though the parties probably will not gain equally. Since the values, beliefs, needs, and thought patterns that are not shared by both parties can cause many unanticipated problems in intercultural negotiation, you have to be constantly very observant of changes from your initial expectations, carefully analyze the differences, and adapt your negotiation strategy accordingly.

11 (Adapted from C. Mitchell *International Business Culture,* Chapter 13)

protocol	礼仪，礼节	cumulative	累积的，累计的
boil down to	归结为	prism	棱镜，棱柱体

Reading Comprehension

Each of the following statements contains information in Text A. Decide whether the statement is true (T) or false (F) based on the text.

1. Negotiating skills are value free and are the same around the world, like the rules of chess for opening moves, middle game, and end game.
2. In the United States, decisions can be made quickly but their implementation may take a long time.
3. The value placed on saving and giving face is closely linked to the powerful theme of preservation of group harmony in Confucian societies as well as deep respect for the existing social order.
4. If you use a common language to negotiate, you may provide documents and contracts in this language as well.

Translation

Translate the following sentences into English.

1. 我们深刻认识到，只有合作共赢才能办成事、办好事、办大事。

____

____

____

2. 和平合作、开放包容、互学互鉴、互利共赢的丝路精神，是共建“一带一路”最重要的力量源泉。

____

____

____

3. 世界现代化应该是和平发展的现代化、互利合作的现代化、共同繁荣的现代化。

____

____

____

Text B

Culture Makes the Business World Go Round

1 Edward Hall, a leader in the field of intercultural studies, famously said, “The single greatest barrier to business success is the one erected by culture.” Can cultural differences have as big an impact on international business ventures as financial planning and visionary leadership? The surprising answer is: Yes!

2 A good example is the role of relationships in business dealings. While relationships play only a minor role in US business culture, they play a major role in Asian, African, and Middle Eastern countries. In these cultures, in varying degrees, relationship building is like a torch that lights and guides the way for business to occur.

3 Let’s take the example of Kevin Johnston, a senior vice-president of a US company specializing in hospitality management. Kevin was put in charge of finalizing a merger with a company in the United Arab Emirates (UAE). Virtually all of the complicated negotiations had been completed. What remained was a 3-day trip to the UAE for face-to-face meetings between the partners to sign the paperwork and close the deal.

4 Kevin was determined that nothing would detain him from succeeding. He sent out a memorandum across his company, enthusiastically

describing the planned merger with the UAE partners. Having compiled all the necessary documents and graphs, with every figure and decimal in place, and having prepared a thorough exposition certifying the quality of his company, he packed his briefcase and headed for the UAE.

5 Kevin arrived in the UAE excited to seal the deal. He was treated with extraordinary hospitality: an elaborate hotel, **blue ribbon** foods, elegant convertibles with drivers to tour the city, a parade of entertainment, and beautiful gifts to commemorate the visit. He tried repeatedly to bring out his files, open the conversation and get down to business. But, surprisingly, for the three days he spent in the UAE, none of his Emirate colleagues seemed ready to hear his financial briefing. Each time Kevin tried to speak about the deal, his prospective partners seemed to "kidnap" the conversation, diverting it to other topics. They would inquire about his health, his family or his views on education and other important issues.

6 Upon leaving the UAE, Kevin felt **exasperated** and defeated. He hadn't been able to receive the thorough interrogation of the materials for which he had so carefully prepared. His progress toward closing the deal was exactly where it was when he left the US: nil.

7 The above case is a classic example of how a friction between different cultural expectations causes delay that, if not handled appropriately, will bring the deal to an abrupt end and leave both sides reeling. The substantial loss of revenue can never be refunded and can leave a struggling company falling without a parachute.

8 Kevin made the mistake of assuming that the "certifications" involved in sealing the deal were in his briefcase. He **charged into** the meetings like a bull. For many cultures, a person's certifications are established not only by their accomplishments, their education and abilities, but also by more personal connections. In this case, the UAE partners wanted to know if Kevin was a good man, a family man, a trustworthy man. This type of rating establishes a trusting relationship for them. Had Kevin patiently taken the time to establish relationships, he would likely have been asked to share his carefully prepared documents and have closed the deal.

9 Sociologists agree that another key aspect influencing global business is the concept of face. Cross-cultural differences in the way we save face impact our perceptions of trust and respect, which in turn impact our relationships and **group cohesion**.

10 Take the example of Ann, a US manager who took a reactionary approach to cultural differences. Ann thought being a nominee for the leadership position with a sales team based in Singapore was a climax of her career. Ann tried to establish a working relationship with each team member. After a few weeks of working on team unification and solidarity, presenting guidelines, and offering sales advice, she carefully compartmentalized goals for each member of the sales team.

11 Later, when the team convened face-to-face for their first quarterly review meeting, Ann, after praising a Chinese team member, boldly criticized and questioned a Korean, trying to extract the exact reason why he was lagging so far behind on his goals. The meeting immediately lost its **groove**. The entire group

became solemn and, for the rest of the meeting, remained polite but largely mute.

12 Clearly, Ann was not familiar with the concept of saving face in other cultures. In US culture, saving face exists — but only minimally, and **tactful** but straightforward speech is highly valued. US managers routinely speak freely about someone else's accomplishments or failures in open, public settings, such as during meetings. This is different in Asian cultures. Singling out an individual due to praise or criticism, a daily habit amongst American managers, may cause Asians to become uncomfortable or deeply embarrassed.

13 Ann needs to consider more culturally appropriate ways to support and motivate her team. Providing feedback, especially negative feedback, in more private settings will be helpful. Most of all, she should work on giving more courteous and supportive praise and encouragement, which will help move toward the unification and cohesion that high functioning teams need in order to be successful.

14 Around the world, deeper structures such as relationship building and face saving **are embedded in** the values, beliefs and behavior of a culture. They are much harder to understand than the glossary of terms in any culture's language phrase book. The advice is: Always ask for clarification and seek new insights. For business success, it is essential to learn to mediate these deeper cultural differences. Though it may be a little complicated to incorporate them into your way of thinking and communicating, it is well worth the effort!

blue ribbon	头等的，一流的	groove	最佳状态，惯例
exasperated	恼怒的，愤怒的，烦恼的	tactful	机智老练的，圆通的，不得罪人的
charge into	冲进，撞上	be embedded in	深植于……，嵌入……
group cohesion	群体凝聚力，团体内聚力		

Reading Comprehension

Choose the best answer to each of the following questions.

1. According to the text, where is relationship building important for business success?
   - ☐ In Europe.
   - ☐ In Asia.
   - ☐ In America.
2. How did Kevin feel before he left for the United Arab Emirates?
   - ☐ He was confident that he could complete the deal.
   - ☐ He was eager to hear the financial report of the UAE company.
   - ☐ he was not satisfied with the documents he had prepared for the meeting.

3. How did Kevin's trip to the UAE end?
- [ ] It was a miracle because he solved all the important issues with little difficulty.
- [ ] It was a disaster because his documents turned out to be incomplete.
- [ ] It was a failure because he didn't close the deal with the UAE company.

4. What accounted for the result of Kevin's trip?
- [ ] He refused to accept any gift and never tried to talk about real business.
- [ ] His UAE partners were not satisfied with his financial report.
- [ ] He knew little about the cultural differences between the US and the UAE.

5. How did Ann handle cultural differences when she led the sales team in Singapore?
- [ ] With great passion for promoting Asian cultural values in the team.
- [ ] With little consideration of the importance of saving face in Asia.
- [ ] By meeting the team members regularly to learn more about Asian culture.

6. What can be inferred from the example about Ann given in the text?
- [ ] Ann was very interested in learning about Asian culture.
- [ ] Asian managers avoid criticizing a person in the face of others.
- [ ] American managers like regular group meetings and private talks.

Text C

Doing Business in Different Cultures

1 **Doing Business in Russia**

2 China and Russia are working closely under the Belt and Road Initiative, and the growing markets in energy sector and e-commerce industry have attracted more enterprises to explore business opportunities. Here are some suggestions for being successful in Russia:

3 1. Build personal relationships with partners. East or West, friendship is best. You cannot always count on business laws and contracts when there are contract disputes, because a lot of time and effort is needed to legally enforce the agreement. Detailed contracts can be **hammered out** later on; in the beginning, all that counts is friendship.

4 2. Use local consultants. Because the rules of business keep changing all the time, it pays to have a local Russian consultant working with the company. Russian expatriates often are not up-to-date on what is going on. So the consultant should be someone from Russia who understands the local business climate.

5 3. Consider business ethics. Ethical behavior is often different in different countries. For example, it is traditional in Russia to give gifts to those with whom one wants to transact business,

an approach that is often regarded as bribery in the United States.

6 4. Be patient. In order to get something done in Russia, it often takes months of waiting. Those who are in a hurry to make quick deal are often sorely disappointed.

7 5. Stress exclusivity. Russians like exclusive arrangements and often negotiate with just one firm at a time. This is in contrast to Western businesspeople, who often "shop" their deals and may negotiate with a half dozen firms at the same time before settling on one.

8 6. Remember that personal relations are important. Russians like to do business face-to-face. So when they receive letters or faxes, they often put them on their desk but do not respond to them. They are waiting for the businessperson to contact them and set up a personal meeting.

9 7. Keep financial information personal. When Westerners enter into business dealings with partners, it is common for them to share financial information with them and to expect the same from the latter. However, Russians wait until they know their partner well enough to feel comfortable before sharing data. Once trust is established, then this information is provided.

10 8. Research the company. In dealing effectively with Russian partners, it is helpful to get information about the company, its management hierarchy, and how it typically does business. This information helps the chances of good relations because it gives the Western partner a basis to know what they stand to gain from entering into the venture.

11 9. Clarify terminology. It is important to double-check and make sure that the other party clearly understands the proposal, knows what is expected and when, is agreeable to the deal.

12 These steps can be critical to the success of a business venture in Russia. They require careful consideration of cultural factors and it often takes a lot longer than initially anticipated. However, the benefits may be worth the wait. And when everything is completed, there is a final cultural tradition that should be observed: fix and reinforce the final agreements with a nice dinner together and an invitation to the Russians to visit your country and see your facilities.

13 **Doing Business in India**

14 Most Indian businesspeople speak English, but many of their values and beliefs are markedly different from those in the West. Thus, understanding Indian culture is critical to doing business in India. When doing business in India, some useful customs to know include:

15 1. It is important to be on time for meetings.

16 2. Personal questions should not be asked unless the other individual is a friend or close associate.

17 3. Titles are important, so people who are doctors or professors should be addressed accordingly.

18 4. Public displays of affection are considered to be inappropriate, so one should refrain from backslapping or touching others.

19 5. Beckoning is done with the palm turned down, while pointing often is done with the chin.

20 6. When eating or accepting things, use the right hand, because the left is considered to be unclean.

21 7. The namaste gesture can be used to greet people; it is also used to convey other messages, including a signal that one has had enough food.

22 8. Bargaining for goods and services is common; this contrasts with Western traditions, where bargaining might be considered rude or **abrasive**.

23 It is important to remember that Indians are very tolerant of outsiders and understand that many are unfamiliar with local customs and procedures. Therefore, there is no need to make a phony attempt to conform to Indian cultural traditions. Making an effort to be polite and courteous is sufficient.

24 **Doing Business in Arab Countries**

25 Businesspeople from Western cultures often find it extremely hard to do business in Arab countries, and a number of Arab cultural characteristics can be cited for this difficulty.

26 One is the Arab view of time. It is common to use the cliché "time is money" for many cultures to view time. In Arab countries, however, a favorite expression is *Bukrainsah Allah*, which means "tomorrow if God wills", an expression that explains the Arab's fatalistic approach to time. Arabs believe that Allah controls time, in contrast to Westerners, who believe they control their own time. As a result, if Arabs commit themselves to a date in the future and fail to show up, there is no guilt or concern on their part, because they have no control over time in the first place.

27 Another Arab cultural belief that generally holds is that destiny depends more on the will of a supreme being than on the behavior of individuals. A higher power **dictates** the outcome of important events, so individual action is of little consequence. This thinking affects not only Arab's aspirations but also their motivation. Also of importance is that the status of Arabs largely is determined by family position and social contact and connections, not necessarily by their own accomplishments. This view helps to explain why some Middle Easterners take great satisfaction in appearing to be helpless. In fact, helplessness can be used as a source of power, for in this area of the world, the strong are resented and the weak compensated.

28 Arabs also make wide use of elaborate and ritualized forms of greetings and leave-taking. A businessperson may wait far past the assigned meeting time before being admitted to an Arab's office. Once there, the individual may find a host of others present. Moreover, during the meetings, there may be continuous interruptions, visitors may arrive and begin talking to the host, and messengers may come in and go out on a regular basis. The businessperson is expected to take all this activity as perfectly normal and remain composed and ready to continue discussion as soon as the host is prepared to do so.

29 Business meetings typically conclude with an offer of coffee or tea. This is a sign that the meeting is over and that future meetings, if there are to be any, should now be arranged.

30 Unlike the case in many other countries,

titles are not in general use on the Arabian Peninsula, except in the case of royal families, ministers, and high-level military officers. Additionally, initial meetings typically are used to get to know the other party. Business-related decisions may not occur until the third or fourth meeting. Also, in contrast to the common perception among many Western businesspeople who have never been to an Arab country, it is not necessary to bring the other party a gift. If this is done, however, it should be a modest gift. A good example is a novelty or souvenir item from the visitor's home country.

31 Arabs attach a great deal of importance to status and rank. When meeting with them, one should pay **deference** to the senior person first. It also is important never to criticize or **berate** anyone publicly. This causes the individual to lose face, and the same is true for the person who makes these comments. Mutual respect is required at all times.

32 Other useful guidelines for doing business in Arab cultures include:

33 1. It is important never to display feelings of superiority, because this makes the other party feel inferior. No matter how well someone does something, the individual should let the action speak for itself and not brag or put on a show of self-importance.

34 2. One should not take credit for joint efforts. A great deal of what is accomplished is a result of group work, and to indicate that one accomplished something alone is a mistake.

35 3. Much of what gets done is a result of going through administrative channels in the country. It often is difficult to **sidestep** a lot of this red tape, and efforts to do so can be regarded as disrespect for legal and governmental institutions.

36 4. Connections are extremely important in conducting business. Well-connected businesspeople can get things done much faster than their counterparts who do not know the ins and outs of the system.

37 5. Patience is critical to the success of business transactions. Time consideration should be built into all negotiations, thus preventing one from giving away too much in an effort to reach a quick settlement.

38 6. Important decisions are usually made in person, not by correspondence or telephone. This is why your personal presence is often a prerequisite for success in the Arab world. Additionally, while there may be many people who provide input on the final decision, the ultimate power rests with the person at the top, and this individual will rely heavily on personal impressions, trust, and **rapport.**

hammer out （经长时间或艰难的讨论）达成，敲定（协议或条约）	berate 斥责，痛斥
abrasive 生硬粗暴的，伤人感情的	sidestep 回避，规避
dictate 支配，决定	rapport 融洽，和谐
deference 尊敬，遵从	

Discussion

Based on the description of doing business in different countries, analyze the cultural dimensions of Russia, India and Arab countries according to Hofstede's theory.

Suggestions for Further Reading

Unit 9

Barriers to Effective Intercultural Communication

However objective and uniform we want to make organizations, they will not have the same meaning for individuals from different cultures.

— Fons Trompenaars

Learning Objectives

At the end of this unit, you should be able to:

- understand some barriers caused by emotional problems;
- comprehend some barriers caused by attitudinal problems;
- analyze various reasons for the persistence of ethnocentrism, stereotyping, prejudice and racism.

Warm-up Activities

1 Case Study I

Liu Jun, a Chinese who works with a British boss, Mr. Wright, wants to take a leave to take his mom to see a doctor. The following is Liu Jun's conversation with his boss.

Liu: Mr. Wright.

Mr. Wright: Yes?

Liu: My mother is not very well, sir.

Mr. Wright: So?

Liu: She has to go to hospital.

Mr. Wright: Well, go on with it. What do you want?

Liu: She has to go to hospital on Thursday.

Mr. Wright: Bloody hell, man. What do you want?

Liu: Nothing, Mr. Wright.

Questions:

1. What does Liu Jun want and why does he finally give it up?
2. What is the cause to the misunderstanding between Liu Jun and his boss?

2 Case Study II

A British general manager upon arrival in Thailand refused to take his predecessor's car. The Thai finance manager asked the new GM what type of Mercedes he would like, then, the GM asked for a Suzuki or a Mini, anything that could be handled easily in the congested traffic in Bangkok.

Three weeks later the GM called the finance manager and asked about prospects for the delivery of his car. The Thai lost his reserve for a moment and exclaimed, "We can get you a new Mercedes by tomorrow, but Suzuki takes much, much longer." The GM asked him to see what he could do to speed up the process. After four weeks the GM asked to see the purchase order for the car. The purchasing department replied that, because it would take so long to get a small car, they had decided to order a Mercedes.

The GM's patience had run out. At the first management meeting he brought the issue up and asked for an explanation. Somewhat shyly, the predominantly Thai management team explained that they could hardly come to work on bicycle.

Questions:

1. Why did the GM have difficulties in getting a Suzuki or Mini?
2. Why did the management team say they could hardly come to work on bicycle?

Text A

Emotional Problems as Barriers to Intercultural Communication

1 At the very beginning of this book (Unit 1), obstacles to effective intercultural communication were briefly introduced. In this unit, we will have a closer look at some universal barriers.

2 In the process of intercultural communication, we do not always undergo smooth experiences. In a lot of cases, we may have communication problems, which may **hinder** our interactions with people from other cultures; we call them cultural barriers or obstacles. Cultural barriers are challenges to cross-cultural communication within an organization. Cultural diversity makes communication difficult as the mindset of people of different cultures are different, the language, signs and symbols are also different. Different cultures have different meaning of words, behaviors and gestures. Among these hindrances, emotional problems are very obvious.

3 **Anxiety and Uncertainty**

4 Do you feel anxious and uncertain when you communicate with people from other cultures? The answer might possibly be yes. Actually, such kind of feeling may happen in almost any intercultural communication case.

5 Anxiety refers to the feeling of not knowing what one is expected to do, and focusing on that feeling and not being totally present in the communication transaction. It is the state of feeling nervous, which can affect communication when one focuses so much on his own feelings that he does not pay attention to what other people are telling him. Anxiety may also affect one's ability to communicate his ideas to others, for he pays too much attention to his uncomfortable feelings.

6 For example, people may have experienced anxiety on their first day on a new college campus or in a new job. They may be so conscious of being new — and out of place — and focus so much of their attention on that feeling that they make common mistakes and appear awkward to others.

7 Uncertainty refers to our **cognitive** inability to explain our own or others' feelings and behaviors in interactions because of an ambiguous situation that evokes anxiety. Being uncertain means being unsure about what the future will hold for oneself and one's situation.

Anxiety happens because of being afraid of failure in communication events, while uncertainty happens because we are unable to predict others' ideas and behaviors. Whatever intercultural communication events we are involved in, we are likely to suffer from anxiety and uncertainty, which hinder effective communication to varying degrees.

8 **Assuming Similarity Instead of Difference**

9 The second barrier is assuming similarity instead of difference. It refers to the idea that people coming from another culture are more similar to you than they actually are or that another person's situation is more similar to yours than it in fact is. It's true that we are more comfortable being around people who have similar outlooks, habits and traits. It's a natural inclination to seek topics that both parties find interesting, and if enough commonality can be found, it is equally likely for friendship to form and involve.

10 When an individual does not know about a new culture, he might assume there are no differences to behave in the new culture as he would in his home culture. When communicating with people from another culture, this individual who assumes similarities when differences actually exist, is likely to regard and treat other people as "his people" and to assume there must be only one way of doing things: that is "his way".

11 However, each culture is different and unique to some degree. Culture separates a person from people with a history different from his own. If a person assumes that the display of emotions by people from other cultures is similar to that of his own culture, he might see people in some situations as lacking emotions or others in other situations as displaying emotions inappropriately.

12 The bias for similarity poses a potential problem when engaging in communication with someone of a different culture who may look, act, speak, and think differently from you. Overcoming that bias requires making an extra effort to appreciate and understand those differences.

hinder 阻碍，妨碍	inclination 倾向，倾斜度，趋向
cognitive 认识的，感知的	

Exercises

The purpose of this questionnaire is to help you assess the amount of anxiety and uncertainty you generally experience when you communicate with strangers. Respond to each statement by indicating the degree to which the adjectives are applicable when you interact with strangers. If you never have the experience, answer 1 in the space provided; if you almost never have the experience, answer 2; if you sometimes have the experience and sometimes do not, answer 3; if you almost always have the experience, answer 4; if you always have the experience, answer 5.

_________ 1. I am not confident when I communicate with strangers.

_________ 2. I can interpret strangers' behavior when we communicate.

_________ 3. I am indecisive when I communicate with strangers.

_________ 4. I can explain strangers' behavior when we communicate.

_________ 5. I am not able to understand strangers when we communicate.

_________ 6. I know what to do when I communicate with strangers.

_________ 7. I am uncertain how to behave when I communicate with strangers.

_________ 8. I can comprehend strangers' behavior when we communicate.

_________ 9. I am not able to predict strangers' behavior when we communicate.

_________ 10. I can describe strangers' behavior when we communicate.

To find your scores, first reverse the responses for the even-numbered items (if you wrote 1, make it 5; if you wrote 2, make it 4; if you wrote 3, leave it as 3; if you wrote 4, make it 2; if you wrote 5, make it 1). Next, add the numbers next to each of the items. Scores range from 10 to 50. The higher your score, the more anxiety and uncertainty you experience when interacting with others.

(Adapted from W. B. Gudykunst, *Bridging Differences*. Califonia: Sage Publications, 1994)

Text B

Attitudinal Problems as Barriers to Intercultural Communication

1 Besides the above-mentioned emotional problems, there are still some typical and common attitudinal problems that handicap people in intercultural communication. Culture also gives rise to prejudices, ethnocentrism, manners and opinions.

2 **Ethnocentrism**

3 People tend to evaluate all other cultures by their own self-reference criterion. For this reason, their evaluations can lead to **complacency** and are often accompanied by feelings of dislike, or even hostility to other cultures.

4 **Stereotypes**

5 A stereotype is a generalization or a mental categorizing of groups in certain cultures, especially when applied to something unfamiliar or complex. Stereotyping is often dangerous and fraught with limitations.

6 **Prejudice**

7 Prejudice refers to an **antipathy** based on faulty and inflexible generalizations

(stereotypes). It's often accompanied by suspicion, fear, contempt, or even hatred.

8 **Racism**

9 Racism is any policy, practice, belief, or attitude that attributes characteristics or status to individuals based on their race. Racism involves not only prejudice, but also the exercise of power over individuals based on their race. Racism can be conscious or unconscious, intentional or unintentional.

10 Racism exists worldwide and some experts believe that racism may be difficult to **eradicate**, because "race" is linked to physical differences among peoples, and such features as dark skin color have been seen as markers of low status. At the cultural level, racism denies the existence of the culture of a particular group; for example, the denial that African Americans represent a unique and distinct culture that is separate from both European American culture and all African cultures. Cultural racism also involves the rejection by one group of the beliefs and values of another, such as the "negative evaluations by whites of black cultural values".

11 In summary, the above four levels often occur together, with ethnocentrism at the center, contributing to intercultural barriers such as stereotypes, prejudice, racism (Table 9.1).

Table 9.1 Attitudinal Problems in Intercultural Communication

Categories	Features	Examples
Ethnocentrism	Inherent beliefs of the superiority of one's own ethnic group or culture over others'	My nation is best in almost every aspect.
Stereotypes	Wrong or set ideas about certain groups or persons from another culture	Japanese people are extremely polite and obedient but distrustful of foreigners. They bow extensively and are very good business people.
Prejudice	Usually a feeling rooted in suspicion, fear, or intolerance	African people are lazy and often late for work. They are uncultured people with no respect to others.
Racism	Limitation of low-status races to low-status jobs or enslavement and be excluded from access to political power, economic resources, and unrestricted civil rights	Survey finds that patients of color more often brace for unfair treatment in health care.

12 **Reasons for the Persistence of Ethnocentrism, Stereotyping, Prejudice and Racism**

13 When studying ethnocentrism, stereotyping, prejudice, and racism, people may be struck with the role that communication can play in either spreading the beliefs or stopping their spread. Ethnocentrism, stereotyping, prejudice and racism are commonly viewed as being rooted in the child's early socialization and fostered in communication with other people who are prejudiced or discriminative.

14 Researchers have suggested various reasons for the persistence of ethnocentrism, stereotyping, prejudice and racism.

15 **Socialization**

16 Ethnocentrism, stereotyping, prejudice and racism are learned. Many of them are passed on from parents to children, sometimes in

subtle messages such as "we don't associate with people like that" or "be careful when you are with them".

17 **Social Benefits**

18 Expressing ethnocentrism, stereotyping, prejudice and racism may bring support from others who share them. For example, it is difficult for people to break away from the prejudices of their families and friends, as rejecting the prejudice can be perceived as breaking away from the association.

19 **Economic Benefits**

20 Ethnocentrism, stereotyping, prejudice and racism can be strong when there is direct competition for jobs. When Chinese immigrants worked on building the transcontinental railroad across the United States when jobs were plentiful, Chinese were perceived as hardworking, industrious, and law-abiding. But after the railroad was completed and jobs **dwindled**, Chinese were perceived as crafty and stupid.

21 Psychological Benefits

22 Ethnocentrism, stereotyping, prejudice and racism can be used to generate a feeling of superiority and to explain a complex world in terms of simple causes as in saying "those people are the source of all our problems".

complacency	自满，自鸣得意，自得	eradicate	根除，消灭，杜绝
antipathy	厌恶，反感	dwindle	（逐渐）减少，缩小，变小

Reading Comprehension

Each of the following statements contains information in Text B. Decide whether the statement is true (T) or false (F) based on the text.

1. Ethnocentrism, stereotyping, prejudice and racism are learned.
2. Although stereotypes are considered as being negative judgments, they can also be positive.
3. When communicating with people from other cultures, an individual sometimes is likely to treat them as "his people" and to assume there is only one way of doing things: that is "his way".
4. Assumption of superiority may lead to assuming similarity instead of difference.
5. Economy is not the reason for the persistence of ethnocentrism, stereotyping, prejudice and racism.

Banked Cloze

Fill in the blanks by selecting suitable words from the word bank. You may not use any of the words more than once.

A. ethnocentrism	B. stereotypes	C. direct	D. appreciate
E. different	F. indirect	G. miscommunication	H. indifferent

1. ____________ occurs due to different beliefs, values, or behavioral patterns.

2. Looking down on other cultures and believing them to be deficient in some way is called ____________.

3. Statements like "All women love to shop", "All men like sports", "All accountants are boring", and "All New Yorkers are open-minded" are based on ____________.

4. People are very______________because they value free speech and express their personal opinions openly and assertively, saying exactly what they mean.

5. In order to promote human understanding and successful interaction among people from diverse cultures, one must ____________ and value cultural differences.

6. No culture is better than another; it is simply____________.

Text C

More about Attitudinal Barriers

1 **Ethnocentrism**

2 Ethnocentrism is derived from the two Greek words *ethnos*, meaning nation, and *kentron*, meaning the center of a circle. "Ethno" is the prefix denoting cultural, ethnic, or racial groupings; "centrism" refers to the centrality of our own group. Ethnocentrism means that we hold views and standards that are "own group centric" and make judgments about other groups based on our own group's values and beliefs. In the context of the Greek culture in the Golden Age, for example, those who spoke the Greek language were viewed as the "cultured" and "eloquent" people, while those who did not speak the language of Greece were labeled as *barbarikos*, or "barbarians" (i.e. those "aliens" whose language was incomprehensible and sounded like a repeated babbling "barbar" noise). When rigidly held views take on an in-group **favoritism** stance, the sentiments of in-group superiority and out-group inferiority are reinforced.

3 Another example of this ethnocentric tendency can be found in the Chinese characters for "China" (or "Middle Kingdom"). The characters or pictographs for "China", first written more than 4,000 years ago during the Hsia Dynasty, meant "the center of the universe". This example is also reminiscent of the concept of "Manifest Destiny" that prevailed in the United States during the 19th century. Finally, we only need to look at any world atlas, as produced by each nation, to understand the ethnocentric perspective: every nation shows itself in a central position on the map, with neighboring states depicted as **peripheral**.

4 Ethnocentrism is our defensive attitudinal tendency to view the values and norms of our culture as superior to other cultures, and we perceive our cultural ways of living as the most reasonable and proper ways to conduct our lives. Consequently, there is the expectation that all other groups should follow our civilized ways of thinking and behaving. Ethnocentrism is **bolstered** through our own cultural socialization process. It can consist of both implicit and explicit attitudes toward out-group members' customs or behavior. Ethnocentrism is summarized as the "view of things in which one's own group is the center of everything, and all others are rated and scaled with reference to it". **Harry Triandis** explains that all human beings display the ethnocentric tendencies to (1) define what goes on in their cultures as "natural" and "correct" and what goes on in other cultures as "unnatural" and "incorrect"; (2) perceive in-group values, customs, norms, and roles as universally valid — that is, what is good for us is good for everybody; (3) act in ways that favor the in-group and exalt it; and (4) experience relational distance from the out-group especially when one's membership identity is threatened or under attack.

5 While all human beings carry a certain degree of ethnocentric tendency in them because of their needs for identity security, in-group inclusion, and predictability, a rigidly held ethnocentric mindset creates a superior-inferior gap in intergroup relations. The degree of ethnocentric tendency in an individual can range all the way from the basic need for valued social identity to the identity defensive need for power or dominance. Additionally, people can be ethnocentric about different aspects of their culture (e.g., language, food, architecture). Under conditions of a perceived out-group threat of competition for scarce resources, members of various identity groups can oscillate between high ethnocentrism and low ethnocentrism depending on the changing circumstances.

6 Everyone is vulnerable to ethnocentrism — **sojourners**, immigrants, and even members of the host culture. A sojourner with feelings of ethnocentrism can expect to encounter difficulties adjusting to a new set of cultural norms. Taken to an extreme, ethnocentrism can lead to prejudice, which in turn can produce mistrust, hostility, and even hate.

7 A stereotype is a fixed notion about persons in a certain category, with no distinctions made among individuals. In other words, it is an overgeneralized and oversimplified belief we use to categorize a group of people.

8 We have a tendency to make a claim that

often goes beyond the facts, with no valid basis. Stereotypes may be based on the truth, but they are exaggerated statements regarding our belief about what a group of people are or should be. For example, imagine that your wallet was stolen by "a" Korean when you were traveling in Korea last summer. The incident ruined your whole trip there. When you came back, your friends asked how your trip to Korea was. You might have said, "Those Koreans are thieves. They stole my wallet." This is an example of stereotyping.

9 We form stereotypes in three ways. First, we may categorize people or things by the most obvious characteristics they possess. For example, I asked a Japanese student about her first impression of the United States of America. She said, "Wow! Everything is big here."

10 Following are the first impressions of the United States of a group of Japanese visitors.

1. Americans walk very fast.
2. Americans are always in a hurry.
3. Americans are wasteful in utilizing space.
4. Americans always try to talk everything out.
5. Americans are very straightforward in talking.
6. American students ask too many questions in the classroom and don't respect professors.

11 Second, we may apply a set of characteristics to a whole group of people. For example, you may hear someone say that Americans eat hotdogs and wear cowboy boots.

12 Third, we may give the same treatment to each member of the group. "You are a Chinese, you must be smart" is stereotyping. The following are common stereotypes of Americans:

1. Americans are rich.
2. Americans drive big cars.
3. Americans talk a lot but say little.
4. Americans have superficial relationships.
5. Americans do not care about old people.
6. Americans think only about money.
7. Americans are outgoing and friendly.
8. Americans lack discipline.
9. Americans are disrespectful of age and status.
10. Americans are ignorant of other countries.
11. Americans are extravagant and wasteful.
12. Americans are loud, rude, boastful, and immature.

13 Stereotypes may vary along four dimensions: direction, intensity, accuracy, and content. The direction of stereotypes refers to the positive / favorable and negative / unfavorable aspects of statements. We might say that Americans are honest, friendly, hardworking, and ambitious. We might also say that Americans are aggressive, lacking discipline, or don't care about old people. The intensity of a stereotype indicates the strength of a belief about a group of people. "African Americans are very musical" is an example of an intense stereotype. Stereotypes also vary in their accuracy. Although stereotypes are exaggerated and overgeneralized beliefs, they are not always false. Some of them may be half-truths, and others may be partially inaccurate. Finally, stereotypes may vary in their specific content, for example, in the specific traits attributed to a group of people. For example, some African Americans may view white Americans according to a range of traits:

aggressive, biased, cold.

14 Stereotypes naturally develop from a set of oversimplified beliefs into a rigid attitude toward a group of people. Such an attitude based on erroneous beliefs or preconceptions is called prejudice. Stereotypes and prejudice often occur together. In other words, when we hold beliefs (stereotypes), for example, about Italians, we also tend to have prejudice toward them. While beliefs refer to the likelihood that a group of people possesses certain characteristics, they contribute to the formation of attitude systems that directly affect the way we treat the group of people. Thus, prejudice is a learned tendency by which we respond to a given group of people or event in a consistent (usually negative) way. When cognitions (stereotypes) are assigned values (prejudice), we may enact biased action (e. g., racism).

15 Prejudice varies principally along the dimension of intensity. Five common forms of prejudice can be identified in terms of intensity: verbal abuse, physical avoidance, racism, physical attack, and massacre. Examples of the latter include the following:

16 Verbal abuse is often accompanied by ethnic jokes and name-labeling.

1. Dead Indians are good Indians.
2. Japanese = Japs.
3. Blacks = Negroes.
4. Polish = Polacks.

17 Physical avoidance occurs when we dislike a group of people. Because of different religious beliefs, language systems, and behavioral patterns, we may intentionally avoid making friends, going out, studying, or working with certain people. For instance, some Irish Catholics and Protestants have been outcast for dating one another.

18 Racism refers to the denial of equal opportunities to out-group members. Racism often occurs in the areas of employment, residential housing, political rights, educational and recreational opportunities, and other social privileges. Historically, some black and white Americans determined who could join a political party by judging whether a person's skin tone was lighter than the color of a paper bag that hung at the door.

19 As the degree of racism intensifies, physically punishing the group of people who are disliked becomes inevitable. In an eighteen-month period some fifty African American churches were burned down, mainly from arson. At the same time, African Americans in New York City tried to drive Korean merchants from black neighborhoods by means of intimidation. Finally, the worst result of prejudice is massacre. The genocidal slaughter by Hitler of the Jewish people and the burning of women as witches in colonial Americans are two examples. The conflict in **Rwanda** in 1990s also reflects the tendency of ethnic groups to exterminate each other because of different beliefs.

20 As we mentioned above, stereotypes and prejudice do not suddenly appear when we are born. We gradually develop our stereotypes and prejudices through the process of learning and socialization. As children, we learn stereotypes from our parents and friends. As we grow up, we learn them from our

schools, churches, friends, and significant others. We also develop stereotypes from our personal experiences, especially through the interactions with people who had visible and distinct traits such as impairment, physical appearance, and skin color. Finally, mass media also play an important role in the development of stereotypes and prejudice. For example, television, radio, books, newspapers, magazines, and films often portray most groups in our society with an overgeneralized and oversimplified view that directly fosters certain kinds of images we form of a group of people.

21 Because stereotypes and prejudice are based on our belief and attitude systems, they affect the way we communicate in intercultural encounters. They may prevent us from interacting with people of different backgrounds; they tend to produce negative feelings during the interactions; and they can lead to unnecessary conflicts when they are intense. To solve the problems of stereotypes and prejudice, we suggest that empathy is the main communication skill we should learn. Empathic persons know how to show understanding by projecting themselves into their partner's position. This means that to be empathic in intercultural interactions, we need to be open-minded in terms of information sharing, to be imaginative in correctly drawing the picture of other's situation, and to show a commitment or strong willingness to understand our culturally different partners in any kind of situation.

(Adapted from Chen Guoming, W. J. Starosta, *Foundations of Intercultural Communication*, Chapter 3)

favoritism 偏爱，偏袒，得宠	bolster 加强，提高
peripheral 周边的，次要的	sojourner 旅居者
Harry Triandis (1926—2019) 哈里·蔡安迪斯，曾任伊利诺伊大学香槟分校心理学系荣誉退休教授（他被认为是跨文化心理学的先驱，其研究重点是不同文化中的认知，如态度、规范和价值观等）	Rwanda 卢旺达共和国（简称“卢旺达”，非洲中东部国家。本文提到的卢旺达冲突是指 1994 年卢旺达的胡图族和图西族之间爆发的暴力冲突。胡图族政府在该国进行了种族灭绝行动，导致了 80 万~100 万人的死亡）

Banked Cloze

Fill in the blanks by selecting suitable words from the word bank. You may not use any of the words more than once.

A. persist	B. eliminate	C. perspective	D. equity	E. involve with
F. social	G. error	H. diverse	I. bring back	J. at the root of

Building a society recognizing and respecting people of different backgrounds and experiences becomes more important today. It is reaffirmed by the inequities shown in some [1] ____________ events. Some racial biases like "microaggressions" to African Americans were [2] ____________ to the forefront by incident such as the killing of George Floyd. Therefore, a long-term commitment should be taken to address inequities that [3] ____________ especially for women and people of color. To create changes and realize social justice, we must do our utmost to [4] ____________ negative influences on our social progression by embracing diversity and inclusion. Diversity is [5] ____________ innovation and technological advancement. Failure to consider [6] ____________ users and consumers resulted in problems such as incidents in the auto industry, high [7] ____________ rate in facial recognition, etc. If diverse design teams are [8] ____________ such projects, we are sure to have better outcomes with the products. So, we need to think more about diversity, [9] ____________ and inclusion and think of working with diverse [10] ____________ to benefit the society.

Exercises

Form groups of three. Suppose these groups are going to participate in the National College Students' Intercultural Competence Contest. Make up stories and act out short plays to show that even the positive stereotypes may be sweet poison.

Discussion

Do you think being ethnocentric equals to being patriotic? Why or why not?

Suggestions for Further Reading

Unit 10

Cultural Adaptation and Intercultural Competence

Understand the differences; act on the commonalities.

— Andrew Masondo

Learning Objectives

At the end of this unit, you should be able to:

- learn to adjust in a new culture more effectively and develop skills for cultural reentry;
- define the components of intercultural communication competence;
- know the basic techniques to improve your intercultural communication competence.

Warm-up Activities

Case Study

Emily is an American representative for a retail company who is looking to place an order for some merchandise made in China. She has been instructed by her boss to start a video call with the company's liaison in China to discuss buying options at her convenience. Emily conducts little research on Chinese communication beliefs and customs and decides to call the next morning. In addition to the linguistic barrier present in the communication between Emily and the company liaison, Emily has failed to acknowledge that although it may be eight in the morning for her; it is seven o'clock at night for the liaison. In China, workdays typically end around six in the evening. Further, Emily does not conduct herself in a formal manner or participate in any greeting ritual to begin the communication, which may be interpreted in Chinese culture as a sign of disrespect.

Questions:

1. What should Emily have done to get more positive receive by Chinese peers?
2. What lesson can you learn from Emily's experience?

Text A

Managing Culture Shock and Engaging in Cultural Adaptation

1 Cultural adaptation is used to define the specific capacity of human beings and human societies to overcome changes of their natural and social environment by modifications to their culture. As mentioned in Unit 6, if you travel to a new culture for the first time, it is likely that you will experience some kind of culture shock. Especially for students who study abroad, the shock could grow intense after the honeymoon stage. Sofia Cussotto, who grew up and finished her Master's Degree study in Italy, experienced culture shock in Ireland working for her PHD when she had no idea what culture shock was. When she moved to France, she had again the shock feeling when she realized the problem and did some research to know culture shock and wrote an article online to share with others who may have similar experience. Culture shock might influence a person's mental health in various

ways, and difficulties adjusting to the new culture can lead to disorientation, confusion and significant psychological distress.

2 Like Sofia Cussotto, many future researchers face a crucial aspect of a career path in the scientific field — mobility. Funding opportunities for researchers usually encourage flexibility and mobility in that they may gain skills and experience by working in different countries, different laboratories and by taking part in international collaborations. To manage successfully the culture shock and adapt to the new culture as soon as possible can help students and researchers abroad improve work efficiency and make more academic achievements.

3 Successful management of culture shock depends on an awareness of its symptoms and the degree of its severity. Sometimes people falsely attribute their problems to sources other than culture shock and there is a tendency to deny that one is experiencing it. In fact, one should accept the fact that virtually all **atypical** problems that occur during acculturation are caused by or **exacerbated** by culture shock.

4 The following suggestions provide some insights into surviving culture shock and developing intercultural adaptation.

5 **1. Learn about the Host Culture and Its Language**

6 Read about your new culture, attend seminars, rent films, and socialize with host nationals about their culture. It's better that you know about the food, dress pattern, beliefs and practices, likes and dislikes of the people of the proposed destination before your travel.

7 Read travel guides, travel tips, and try to find out some social survival skills, such as how to address people in different social groups, how gender roles affect social relationships, what constitutes acceptable behavior in a range of everyday situations, and how gestures and body language differ from your own country. If possible, interview friends or colleagues who have traveled or lived in the culture.

8 Familiarize yourself with the verbal and nonverbal language of your host culture. Practicing functional and frequently used phrases will help you perform basic survival tactics. Keep in mind that common verbal colloquialisms can be wildly misinterpreted across cultures. Find out nonverbal mannerisms and expectations for personal space, time, gestures, and so forth. Learn some appropriate verbal and nonverbal formalities of greeting rituals.

9 **2. Stay Connected to Your Own Culture**

10 After arriving at the new country, spend time with people from your culture, which can reduce the stress of managing life in another culture. Try to know your neighbors, colleagues, schoolmates and whoever relevant to you in the new culture. Besides, read a local newspaper, TV program or website, and find out what the topical issues are.

11 **3. Assume the Principle of Difference**

12 Try to understand that things are simply going to be different in your new culture and that the way you are accustomed to doing things is not the only way. Remember that your perceptual context is biased in favor of your culture and your in-group. How you perceive your host culture is not objective or neutral. All of the verbal and nonverbal messages encoded

and decoded are filtered through your cultural, environmental, socio-relational, and perceptual filters. These filters bias and color your expectations, which will certainly be violated as you interact with your host culture.

13 **4. Anticipate Failure**

14 Regardless of how well you prepare for your journey, there will be moments when you are unsuccessful at accomplishing your goals. Before you depart, anticipate failure events. After your arrival, remember that the freshness cannot last long and misunderstanding will be unavoidable. You're not alone to experience the culture shock and you will manage it successfully and become a global citizen with intercultural competence.

atypical 非典型的，反常的　　exacerbate 加剧，使恶化，使加重

Exercises

1. You have been working and living in Chile for some time, and have gained a lot of valuable business contacts. You would like to do something nice for one of your Chilean business acquaintances. What do you do?
   - ☐ You invite him to your home for a quiet dinner.
   - ☐ You take him to the best nightclubs for a night of drinking.
   - ☐ You buy a bottle of expensive French wine and give it to him.
2. An Egyptian executive, after entertaining his Canadian guest, offered joint partnership in a business venture. The Canadian, delighted with the offer, suggested they meet again the next morning with their respective lawyers to finalize the details. The Egyptian never arrived. Why?
   - ☐ The Canadian should not have set up the next meeting time so soon.
   - ☐ It is difficult to find a good lawyer in Cairo in such a short time.
   - ☐ The Egyptian interpreted inviting lawyers as a sign of mistrust from the Canadian side.
3. In Brazil, it is considered normal to show up for a social event.
   - ☐ Ten to fifteen minutes early.
   - ☐ Ten to fifteen minutes late.
   - ☐ One to two hours late.
4. An Arab businessman offers you a cup of Arabian coffee at his office. You usually do not drink coffee. You should say,
   - ☐ "No, thank you."
   - ☐ "Thank you, but I do not drink coffee."
   - ☐ "Thank you, " and accept the cup of coffee.

Discussion

Do you think members of a host culture have any responsibilities to make immigrants feel comfortable in the new cultural environment? Why?

Text B

Significance of Intercultural Competence

1 We had our attention on abroad students in Text A and discussed cultural adaptation strategies to cope with the culture shock they encounter in the long duration of study. As the mobility across cultures increases day by day, not only students, but also businessmen, government officials, all have the requirements for instructions of successful intercultural assignments. Lack of intercultural competence means unsuccessful learning experiences, failed business ventures or government projects that have not achieved their objectives.

2 **1. The Economic Imperative (for Intercultural Competence)**

3 The economic success of many developed countries in the global arena increasingly depends on individual and collective abilities to communicate competently with people from other cultures. Clearly, their economic relationships require global interdependence and intercultural competence.

4 **2. The Technological Imperative**

5 Today, the "global village" is an image that is used to describe the web of interconnections that modern technologies have created. Communication media now make it possible to establish virtually instantaneous links to people who are thousands of miles away. Modern transportation systems also contribute to the creation of the global village.

6 **3. The Demographic Imperative**

7 Recent data clearly shows that the United States is now a multicultural society, but the United States is not alone in the worldwide transformation of nations into multicultural societies. Throughout Europe, Asia, South America, and the Middle East, there is an increasing pattern of cross-border movements that is changing the distribution of people across the globe. This demographic imperative requires a heightened emphasis on intercultural competence.

8 **4. The Social Justice Imperative**

9 As early as 1980s, Edward T. Hall stated in *Beyond Culture* that "Despite our faith in technology and our reliance on technological solutions, there are no technical solutions to most of the problems confronting human beings ... until mankind transcends the intellectual limitations imposed by our institutions, our

philosophies, and our cultures". In 21st century, the globalization process makes it more important to understand and appreciate those who differ from us. If we could not understand other cultures or if we have prejudice against their cultural values, we might have lots of misunderstandings, conflicts, quarrels, fights and even bloody wars. Social justice and world peace both depend on intercultural competence.

10 Never in history has there been such mixing of peoples and cultures. Nor will this mixing and blending soon slow. People will continue to migrate to nations that hold the promise of security and a more productive life. Employment is now on a global basis — you have just as much chance of working in London as you do in Shanghai. While globalization has created a truly international economy, political states remain separate. Nations are economically interdependent but separated by political and nationalistic interests. The economic ties lessen the likelihood of large-scale conflict, which leaves only dialogue to resolve the political disputes. Thus, the requirement for intercultural skills will increase during your lifetime. For each individual, the intercultural competence is now more vital than ever.

Discussion

1. Why do we need intercultural competence in modern society?
2. When traveling to Boston and then visiting its Chinatown, you can find there are lots of signs in Chinese and people there speaking Chinese. And also many street signs in other U.S. cities such as New York, Miami, or Honolulu, are in another language in addition to English. Some place has a name different from "normal" English.
   (1) What kind of cultural phenomenon can be reflected in this case?
   (2) Could you give some examples of phenomena similar to this one in American society?
   (3) What can we learn from this case?

Text C

Overcome Intercultural Communication Barriers

1 The previous units have laid foundations for the cultivation of intercultural competence. We are going to give suggestions on avoiding the barriers to achieve effective intercultural communication in this last unit, bringing forth some constructive ways to intentionally foster individual intercultural competence.

2 To avoid the intercultural communication

barriers analyzed in Unit 9 such as anxiety, uncertainty, ethnocentrism and stereotyping, some suggestions by scholars are given as follows:

3 **Managing Anxiety and Uncertainty**

4 Even in the same culture communication, many introverted people may have strong sense of anxiety, let alone the intercultural communication. Being aware that anxiety is the natural response in social contact and the anxiety is closely related to uncertainty.

5 Uncertainty is a potential intercultural communication problem and one that is directly related to the natural inclination to seek similarities. During initial meetings, conversation generally involves efforts to learn about the other person, which helps you reduce the cognitive feelings of uncertainty and increase predictability. In other words, it helps you reduce uncertainty about your communicative interaction and lessen your feelings of **apprehension**. First-time meetings with anyone carry some level of uncertainty, but if the person is from a different ethnic group, that sense of uncertainty and anxiety will be increased. This is especially true when you are unable to anticipate the other person's behaviors or understand the reasons for their actions. Simply stated, uncertainty is magnified when you meet people of cultures different from your own. When engaging with someone of another culture, it is important to realize that the other person will also experience feelings of uncertainty. To help alleviate this mutual sense of uncertainty, William Gudykunst advocates being "mindful". By this, he means assuming an increased awareness of your own behaviors and being more accepting of different practices and perspectives. In other words, Gudykunst is telling us that when we communicate interculturally, we need to be more attentive to the behaviors and what is said both by ourselves and the other party.

6 **Guarding Against Ethnocentrism**

7 As discussed in Unit 9, ethnocentrism is the conviction that one's own culture is superior to other cultures. Everyone is vulnerable to ethnocentrism — sojourners, immigrants, and members of the host culture. A sojourner with feelings of ethnocentrism can expect to encounter difficulties adjusting to a new set of cultural norms. Taken to an extreme, ethnocentrism can lead to prejudice, which in turn can produce mistrust, hostility, and even hate. Host culture members may exhibit feelings of ethnocentrism by developing negative judgements about outsiders who have different cultural traits. This situation can easily create a downward spiral in relations between members of the host culture and sojourners. The best way to facilitate effective adaptation is for all parties to recognize and work to resist the strong pull of ethnocentrism. One way of reducing the potential of ethnocentrism is for individuals to learn how their own culture influences and shapes their beliefs, perceptions, values and behaviors.

8 **Avoiding Stereotypes**

9 Because learning stereotypes, along with culture, begins early in life, it should be obvious that the best time to initiate measures to **circumvent** them is during childhood. Research

has revealed that children who experience positive contact with other groups hold fewer negative stereotypes than children who have not had the opportunity for such contact. Studies also show that positive contact among different groups of children will diminish many of the effects of stereotyping by dispelling fictitious and negative perceptions. Because the stereotypes are so deeply embedded, we usually reject information that runs counter to these inflexible categorizations. However, the employment of flexible stereotyping starts when we become aware that categorizing is a natural tendency — we become more "mindful". This involves being open-minded, receptive to new information, avoiding assigning judgmental opinions, and recognizing that intercultural interactions can produce stress and discomfort.

10 **Avoiding Prejudice**

Avoiding prejudice is neither easy nor simple. As with most aspects of culturally instilled perception, prejudices are learned early and reinforced through repeated exposure. However, research has disclosed two techniques that are often successful in dispelling prejudicial views — personal contact and education.

11 The greater the frequency of positive interaction between in-group and out-group individuals, the lower the level of perceived prejudice. This contact does, however, need to meet certain criteria in order to be successful, with the most important being groups of equal status and cooperation for common goals.

12 From an educational perspective, two types of programs have been found to reduce prejudice. The first centers around what is called multicultural education which focus on presenting the "history and cultural practices of a wide array of racial and ethnic groups". The material is related from the point of view of the minority groups rather than that of the dominant culture. Cultural diversity training, the second type of program, is widely used in business and organizational settings. These programs are designed for all corporate employees, from worker to executives. Objectives are to increase employee cultural awareness, heighten intercultural understanding, create self-awareness of one's own cultural behaviors, and demonstrate the value of cultural diversity. Regardless of the program selected, the explicit goals remain the same — to reduce prejudice through intergroup contact and cross-cultural dialogue.

13 The most fundamental method of decreasing prejudice is being personally mindful. You can examine your own prejudices and work to avoid remarks that could be interpreted from that group. Too often, ethnic jokes or slurs are spoken in jest or in order to feel part of the in-group. In addition to being self-mindful, it is important to make others mindful that you do not use or tolerate prejudicial statements.

14 **Countering Racism**

15 Views about race are often deeply entrenched, especially those learned during childhood, but there are some measures that can help reduce racism:

16 1. Try to be honest: When deciding if you hold any racist views, be truthful with yourself.

Although an easy proposition to write but somewhat difficult to accomplish, confronting personal racist views is an important and necessary first step.

17 2. Object to racist jokes and insults: Although a simple act, this will often take considerable courage, especially when confronting family and close friends. However, it will send a clear message to other people that you condemn racism in any form.

18 3. Respect freedom: Everyone knows that there is no absolute freedom, but the individual freedom within its jurisdiction the equal protection of the laws shouldn't be denied. If we have our freedom to value our race, we should respect other people's freedom to cherish their races as well.

19 4. Examine racism's historical roots: In order fully to comprehend and challenge the adverse impact of racism, we need to be able to understand and explain the origins of racist ideas and why they appeal to some people.

20 Racism, stereotyping, and prejudice are pervasive because they are often acquired early in life and, like much of culture, become part of one's way of seeing the world. But if we are determined and take action, we are certain to overcome these barriers to effective intercultural communication without making irreparable mistakes.

apprehension 担心，忧虑，恐惧　　circumvent 设法回避，绕道旅行

Discussion

1. What relationship links stereotypes, prejudice and racism?
2. How do you understand the statement "Prejudice can never be eliminated because it is so deeply rooted in human nature"?

Text D

Develop Intercultural Competence for a Shared Beautiful World

1 If we could overcome the emotional and attitudinal barriers, we have the prerequisite for effective intercultural communication. By effective we mean that those behaviors lead to the achievement of desired outcomes. Effectiveness and appropriateness compose the social evaluation to judge what behavior or ability can be called competence. The phrase "intercultural competence" typically describes one's effective and appropriate engagement with

cultural differences. Intercultural competence has been studied as residing within a person (i.e., encompassing cognitive, affective, and behavioral capabilities of a person) and as a product of a context (i.e., co-created by the people and contextual factors involved in a particular situation).

2 When we have the strong motivation and knowledge of host culture, then our attitudes and behaviors matter in the intercultural communication.

3 Many attitudes contribute to intercultural communication competence, including tolerance for ambiguity, empathy, and **nonjudgmentalness**.

4 **Tolerance for Ambiguity**

5 It refers to the ease in dealing with situations in which much is unknown. Whether we are abroad or at home, interacting with people who look different from us and who behave in ways that are strange to us requires a tolerance for ambiguity.

6 Tolerance for ambiguity is one of the most difficult things to attain. People have a natural preference for predictability; uncertainty can be disquieting. In other words, if you can handle situations you do not immediately understand, then you probably have a high tolerance for ambiguity.

7 **Empathy**

Empathy refers to the ability to know what it's like to "walk in another person's shoes". Empathic skills are culture-bound. We cannot really view the world through another person's eyes without knowing something about his or her experiences and life.

8 Intercultural communication scholars have attempted to come up with a more culturally sensitive view of empathy. American expert on human communication Ben Broome stresses that, in order to achieve empathy across cultural boundaries, people must have strong relationships and strive for the creation of shared meaning in their interpersonal encounters. In addition, cross-cultural empathy must integrate both thinking and feeling — we must try to understand not only what others say (content) but also how they feel (empathy). Finally, he reminds us that to achieve cross-cultural empathy, we must seek to understand the context of both others' lived experiences and the specific encounters.

9 **Nonjudgmentalness**

10 We might like to think that we do not judge others according to our own cultural frames of reference, but it is very difficult. Therefore, nonjudgmentalism is much easier said than done.

11 The D. I. E. exercise is helpful in developing a nonjudgmental attitude. It involves making a distinction between description (D), interpretation (I), and evaluation (E) in the processing of information. Descriptive statements convey factual information that can be verified through the senses. Interpretive statements attach meaning to the description. Evaluative statements clarify how we feel about something. Only descriptive statements are nonjudgmental.

12 This exercise can help us recognize whether we are processing information on a descriptive, interpretive, or evaluative level. Confusing the different levels can lead to misunderstanding and ineffective communication. It is impossible

to always stay at the descriptive level. But it is important to know when we are describing and when we are interpreting. Most communication is at the interpretive level. The descriptions you might get are not really descriptions; rather, they are interpretations that reflect individual and cultural viewpoints.

13 In addition to tolerance, empathy and nonjudgmentalness, there are still some guidelines for the behavioral skills in communication practice.

14 **Respecting Others**

15 How do you feel when someone belittles you, ignores you, embarrasses you in front of others, or otherwise tends to diminish your sense of self-worth? Your emotions would range from anger to hurt. No one likes to feel belittled. Everyone wants some level of respect and dignity along with a positive self-image. If you don't like to be belittled, then don't belittle others. Confucius said, "Do not do to others what you do not like them to do to you." This demand is universal that respect should be given to every human being regardless of their culture. The United Nations Declaration of Human Rights, written in 1948, avers the following in the first of thirty articles: "Article 1: All human beings are born free and equal in dignity and rights. They are endowed with reason and conscience and should act towards one another in a spirit of brotherhood." From the ethical perspective, this means that during communicative actions, we must display respect for the dignity and feelings of the other person. Confucius also advocated this sense of ethical concern, "Without feelings of respect, what is there to distinguish men from beasts?" In the globalized society, we must reach beyond our own cultural norms and respect the norms of other cultures.

16 **Seeking Similarities**

17 We have the nature to assume similarities but in fact we should try hard to find similarities. The similarities that unite people and that make everyone a part of the globalized society range from the obvious to the subtle. For example, all people share the basic desire to live their lives without external constraint — to be free. There is also a universal link between children and family. All people share the excitement of a new birth. Mating and wanting friendship is a common need. Everyone must eventually face old age, and people are joined in knowing that death is inevitable, a part of life's process. The enjoyment of music and art, in all their many forms, is universal. People are very much alike in many significant ways. In a multicultural world, it is important to recognize these commonalities. As the late Professor Samuel Huntington said, "People in all civilizations should search for and attempt to expand the values, institutions, and practices they have in common with people of other civilizations."

18 **Recognize and Respect Cultural Differences**

19 In addition to finding commonalities among people and cultures, it is equally important to recognize, understand, and respect cultural differences. Culture produces varying beliefs, values, and behaviors. Understanding and respecting those cultural variances enables us to develop an intercultural awareness with an ethical perspective. In short, we must keep in mind that people are both alike and different!

20 Only when we acknowledge that there

are cultural differences can we learn from each other's culture, understand that there are different ways of thinking, doing and saying, then we will respect different cultures and appreciate cultural differences, value each culture's uniqueness and promote shared prosperity.

21 Cultural differences are unavoidable, but cultural conflicts can be avoided, which is also embedded in Chinese culture:

22 Harmonious but Different（和而不同）;

23 Seeking Common Ground, while Reserving Differences（求同存异）.

nonjudgmentalness 不加评判，非评判性 aver 断言，坚称

Banked Cloze

Fill in the blanks by selecting suitable words from the word bank. You may not use any of the words more than once.

Part A

A. Intercultural competence	B. Empathy	C. Tolerance for ambiguity
D. Knowledge	E. Context	F. Nonjudgmentalness

1. ____________ refers to the ability to know what it's like to "walk in another person's shoes".
2. ____________ comprises various cognitive aspects of communication competence; it involves what we know about ourselves and others, and about various aspects of communication.
3. ____________ refers to the ease in dealing with situations in which much is unknown.
4. ____________ refers to all the information in the actual communication setting.
5. ____________ refers to the ability to understand and adapt to the target culture.

Part B

A. appreciate	B. commercial	C. distinguish	D. distinctive	E. endure
F. essential	G. financial	H. illusion	I. intercultural	J. judgmental
K. observable	L. purchase	M. political	N. tolerant	

World travelers today can order a latte at a Starbucks in Mumbai, eat a McDonald's Big Mac in Berlin, drink a Coca-Cola in Nairobi, visit an Apple store in Beijing, [1] ____________ a Toyota Corolla in Cairo, try on a pair of Zara jeans in Moscow, find a Louis Vuitton store in Rio de Janeiro, and connect to *Google.com* almost anywhere in the world. And there is a very good chance that in each city, you will be able to speak English with the salesperson. The internationalization of [2] ____________ activities can give the impression that everyone everywhere has a similar lifestyle and enjoys the same things. However, this is an [3] ____________. Over twenty-five years ago, Bamlund vividly illustrated this double-sided nature of cultures:

If outwardly there is little to [4] ____________ what one sees on the streets of Osaka (Japan) and Chicago — hurrying people, trolleys and busses, huge department stores, blatant billboards, skyscraper hotels, public monuments—beneath the surface there remains great distinctiveness. There is a different organization of industry, a different approach to education, a different role for labor unions, and a contrasting pattern of family life, unique law enforcement and penal practices, contrasting forms of [5] ____________ activity, different sex and age roles. Indeed, most of what is thought of as culture shows as many differences as similarities. The [6] ____________ similarities that Barnlund wrote about not only remain today but also, in many cases, have increased. Yet the cultural differences [7] ____________ and continue to influence interactions.

The need to recognize, [8] ____________, and accept cultural similarities and differences is [9] ____________ to developing a complete and honest intercultural ethical perspective. This perspective will help you better access the potential consequences of your communicative acts and become more [10] ____________ of others. It is appropriate here to recall Thomas Jefferson's advice about accepting differences: "It does me no injury for my neighbor to say there are twenty gods, or no God."

Suggestions for
Further Reading